D1498828

Entrepreneurial Impact: The Role of MIT — An Updated Report

Entrepreneurial Impact: The Role of MIT — An Updated Report

Edward B. Roberts

Massachusetts Institute of Technology
USA
eroberts@mit.edu

Charles E. Eesley

Stanford University
USA
cee@stanford.edu

the essence of knowledge

Boston – Delft

Foundations and Trends® in Entrepreneurship

Published, sold and distributed by:
now Publishers Inc.
PO Box 1024
Hanover, MA 02339
USA
Tel. +1-781-985-4510
www.nowpublishers.com
sales@nowpublishers.com

Outside North America:
now Publishers Inc.
PO Box 179
2600 AD Delft
The Netherlands
Tel. +31-6-51115274

The preferred citation for this publication is Edward B. Roberts and Charles E. Eesley, Entrepreneurial Impact: The Role of MIT — An Updated Report, Foundations and Trends® in Entrepreneurship, vol 7, nos 1–2, pp 1–149, 2011

ISBN: 978-1-60198-478-4
© 2011 Edward B. Roberts

Foundations and Trends® in Entrepreneurship
Volume 7 Issues 1–2, 2011
Editorial Board

Editorial Scope

Foundations and Trends® in Entrepreneurship will publish survey and tutorial articles in the following topics:

- Nascent and start-up entrepreneurs
- Opportunity recognition
- New venture creation process
- Business formation
- Firm ownership
- Market value and firm growth
- Franchising
- Managerial characteristics and behavior of entrepreneurs
- Strategic alliances and networks
- Government programs and public policy
- Gender and ethnicity
- New business financing:

- Business angels
- Bank financing, debt, and trade credit
- Venture capital and private equity capital
- Public equity and IPO's
- Family-owned firms
- Management structure, governance and performance
- Corporate entrepreneurship
- High technology
- Technology-based new firms
- High-tech clusters
- Small business and economic growth

Information for Librarians

Foundations and Trends® in Entrepreneurship, 2011, Volume 7, 6 issues. ISSN paper version 1551-3114. ISSN online version 1551-3122. Also available as a combined paper and online subscription.

Foundations and Trends® in
Entrepreneurship
Vol. 7, Nos. 1–2 (2011) 1–149
© 2011 Edward B. Roberts
DOI: 10.1561/0300000030

the essence of knowledge

Entrepreneurial Impact:
The Role of MIT — An Updated Report

Edward B. Roberts[1] and Charles E. Eesley[2]

[1] David Sarnoff Professor of Management of Technology, MIT Sloan School
of Management, and the Founder and Chair of the MIT Entrepreneurship
Center, USA, eroberts@mit.edu
[2] Assistant Professor, Stanford University Department of Management
Science and Engineering, USA, cee@stanford.edu

Abstract

The ultimate value of this study is to help us understand the economic
impact of the entrepreneurial ventures of university graduates. We
know that some universities play an important role in many economies
through their core education, research and development, and other
spillovers. However, in order to support economic growth through
entrepreneurship, universities must create a culture and programs that
make entrepreneurship widely accessible to students. While MIT's
leadership in developing successful entrepreneurs has been evident
anecdotally, this study — one of the largest surveys of entrepreneur
alumni ever conducted — quantifies the significant impact of MIT's
entrepreneurial ecosystem that supports firm start-ups. Furthermore,

* We thank MIT, the MIT Entrepreneurship Center, the Kauffman Foundation, and Gideon
Gartner for their generous support of our research. An earlier version of this work was
published by the Ewing Marion Kauffman Foundation, Kansas City, Missouri, in February
2009.

while MIT is more unique and unusual in the programs it offers and in its historical culture of entrepreneurship, MIT provides a benchmark by which other institutions can gauge the economic impact of their alumni entrepreneurs. The report also provides numerous examples of programs and practices that might be adopted, intact or modified as needed, by other universities that seek enhanced entrepreneurial development. The Appendix identifies several universities that have carried out surveys of alumni entrepreneurs.

Contents

1

Executive Summary

1.1 Economic Impact of MIT Alumni Entrepreneurs

Research and technology intensive universities, especially via their entrepreneurial spin-offs, have a dramatic impact on the economies of the United States and its 50 states. This report is an in-depth case study, carried out during the past few years, of a single research/technology university, the Massachusetts Institute of Technology (MIT), and of the significant consequences it has helped to produce for the nation and the world via its broad-based entrepreneurial ecosystem. From our extensive data collection and analyses, we conclude that, if the active companies founded by living MIT alumni[1] formed an independent nation, conservative estimates indicate that their revenues would make that nation at least the 17th largest economy in the world. Indeed, a less-conservative direct extrapolation of the underlying survey data boosts the numbers to 25,800 active companies

---

[1] Throughout the report we use the term "alumni" to include both male alumni and female alumnae. Furthermore, "alumni" are defined by the MIT Alumni/ae Association to include all persons who received an "earned" degree from MIT, as well as those who were registered in a degree-granting program for at least one full undergraduate term or two full graduate terms.

(as of the end of 2006) founded by living MIT alumni that employ 3.3 million people and generate annual world revenues of nearly $2 trillion, producing the equivalent of the 11th-largest economy in the world.

A deeper examination determines that those firms that were founded based upon technology drawn from MIT and other universities generate 1.7 million of those jobs and $1.0 trillion of global revenues. Together with the companies based upon non-university technology, the technology-based new firms founded account for 85% of the estimated employment and 92% of the overall global sales impact. Non-technology-based companies founded by MIT alumni create slightly under a half million jobs, important but only 15% of the overall economic consequences arising from MIT alumni entrepreneurs.

The ultimate value of this study is to help us understand the economic impact of the entrepreneurial ventures of university graduates. We know that some universities play an important role in many economies through their core education, research and development, and other spillovers. However, in order to support economic growth through entrepreneurship, universities must create a culture and programs that make entrepreneurship widely accessible to students. While MIT's leadership in developing successful entrepreneurs has been evident anecdotally, this study — one of the largest surveys of entrepreneur alumni ever conducted — quantifies the significant impact of MIT's entrepreneurial ecosystem that supports firm start-ups. Furthermore, while MIT is more unique and unusual in the programs it offers and in its historical culture of entrepreneurship, MIT provides a benchmark by which other institutions can gauge the economic impact of their alumni entrepreneurs. The report also provides numerous examples of programs and practices that might be adopted, intact, or modified as needed, by other universities that seek enhanced entrepreneurial development. The Appendix identifies several universities that have carried out surveys of alumni entrepreneurs.

Our database is from a 2003 survey of all living MIT alumni with additional detailed analyses, including more recent verification and updating of revenue and employment figures from the 2006 records of Compustat (public companies) and Dun & Bradstreet (private

companies). For conservatism of our projections, we have deliberately
excluded from our database all companies in which the MIT alumnus
founder had died by 2003, even if the company still survives, such as
Hewlett-Packard or Intel. Even if the founder is still alive, we have
generally excluded from our numbers those MIT alumni-founded companies that had merged with or been sold to other firms, such as
Digital Equipment Corporation (DEC), which had peak employment of
140,000 people prior to its merger with Compaq in 1998 (and their later
merger with Hewlett-Packard). Nor do the database numbers include
MIT alumni-founded firms that had closed prior to our 2003 survey.
These estimates similarly ignore all companies founded by non-alumni
MIT faculty or staff. Thus, we feel that our overall portrayal of MIT's
entrepreneurial impact is quite conservative. Nor do we examine in
addition to these entrepreneurial spin-offs the impact of MIT-generated
science and technology upon the overall innovation and competitiveness of government and industries that benefit from direct and indirect
transfer of scientific know-how and discoveries emerging from MIT, its
faculty, staff, and graduates.

While the economic estimates we present contain some degrees of
uncertainty, the trends in the numbers are clear. More entrepreneurs
emerge out of each successive MIT graduating class, and they are
starting their first companies sooner and at earlier ages. Over time,
the number of multiple companies founded per MIT entrepreneurial
alumnus has also been increasing, thereby generating dramatically
increased economic impact per graduate. MIT acts as a magnet for
foreign students who wish to study advanced engineering, science and
management, and a large fraction of those students remains in the
United States. Well over half of the firms created by foreign students
who graduate from MIT are located in the United States, generating
most of their economic impact in this country.

Thirty percent[2] of the jobs in the MIT alumni firms are in manufacturing (far greater than the 11% of overall United States jobs that are in
manufacturing) and a high percentage of their products are exported.
In determining the location of a new business, entrepreneurs said that

---

[2] We round off most numbers in this report to the nearest percent.

the quality of life in their community, proximity to key markets, and access to skilled professionals were critical considerations, but almost all located where they had been working or attending university, including near graduate schools other than MIT.

The study reveals that the states benefiting most from jobs created by MIT alumni are Massachusetts (for which we estimate about one million jobs worldwide for the entire population of over 6900 active MIT alumni-founded Massachusetts-headquartered companies), California (estimated at 526,000 jobs from its current approximately 4100 MIT alumni-founded firms), New York (estimated at 231,000 jobs), Texas (estimated at 184,000), and Virginia (estimated at 136,000). A total of 15 other states are likely to have more than 10,000 jobs each and only 11 states seem to have fewer than 1000 jobs from MIT alumni companies.

As a result of MIT, Massachusetts has for many years been dramatically "importing" company founders. The estimated 6900 MIT alumni firms headquartered in Massachusetts generate worldwide sales of about \$164 billion. More than 38% of the software, biotech, and electronics companies founded by MIT graduates are located in Massachusetts, whereas much less than 10% of arriving MIT freshmen are from the state. Not only do MIT alumni, drawn from all over the world, remain heavily in Massachusetts but their entrepreneurial offshoots benefit the state and country significantly. Greater Boston, in particular, as well as northern California and the Northeast, broadly, is home to the largest number of MIT alumni companies; however, a significant number of companies are also in the South, the Midwest, the Pacific Northwest, and Europe. About 30% of MIT's foreign students form companies (in contrast with somewhat more than 20% of MIT's US-born students), of which at least half are located in the United States. Those estimated 2340 firms located in the US but formed by MIT foreign-student alumni employ about 101,500 people.

1.2   The Types of Companies MIT Graduates Create

MIT alumni companies are primarily knowledge-based companies in software, biotech, manufacturing (electronics, instruments, machinery), or consulting (architects, business consultants, engineers). These companies have a disproportionate importance to their local economies because they typically represent advanced technologies and usually sell to out-of-state and world markets. That causes their local employment to be considerably higher per dollar of revenues than for companies whose sales are largely to local markets. The global revenues per employee of MIT alumni-founded firms are far greater than those produced by the average American company. Furthermore, they employ higher skilled as well as higher paid employees. They also tend incidentally to have far lower pollution impact on their local environments.

An important subset of the MIT alumni companies is in software, electronics (including instruments, semi conductors, and computers), and biotech. These firms are at the cutting edge of what we think of as high technology and, correspondingly, are more likely to be planning future expansion than companies in other industries. They export a higher percentage of their products, hold one or more patents, and spend more of their revenues on research and development. (Machinery and advanced material firms share many of these same characteristics but are not nearly as numerous as the electronics, software, and biotech companies.)

More than 900 new MIT alumni companies were founded each year during the decade of the 1990s. However, the bulk of total MIT-generated employment results from the estimated 541 companies of 1000 or more employees who have created about 83% of the jobs. Not surprisingly, most of the larger companies have been in existence for some time; however, many younger entrepreneurs have built sizable companies in a short period of time. One in six of the companies founded by a graduate out of school 15 years or less already has 100 or more employees.

1.3 The MIT Entrepreneurial Ecosystem

Rather than any single or narrow set of influences, what we call the overall MIT "entrepreneurial ecosystem," consisting of multiple education, research, and social network institutions and phenomena, contributes vitally to this outstanding and growing entrepreneurial output. The ecosystem rests upon a long MIT history since its 1861 founding and its evolved culture (and logo) of "Mens et Manus," Latin for "mind and hand." The founding tradition at MIT of valuing useful work resulted in the development of strong ties with industry, including encouraging faculty consulting and even (rather uniquely) faculty entrepreneurship since before the beginning of the 20th century. Over the years, the increasingly evident MIT entrepreneurial environment has attracted entrepreneurship-inclined students, staff, and faculty, leading to a strong positive feedback loop of ever-increasing entrepreneurial efforts.

Alumni initiatives in 1969 and the early 1970s appear to be the first direct institutional moves to encourage entrepreneurship, leading to the establishment of the now worldwide MIT Enterprise Forum. Since its beginning, the Cambridge, Massachusetts chapter alone has helped nurture more than 700 young companies, with equivalent numbers across the rest of the country. Beginning in 1990, the MIT Entrepreneurship Center crystallized these efforts over the past 20 years by launching more than 30 new entrepreneurship courses at MIT and by assisting in the formation and growth of a large number of related student clubs. The resulting dramatic increase in networking among students across all MIT departments and schools, and between the students and the surrounding entrepreneurship and venture capital community, appears in survey results to be the primary MIT-related factor influencing the growth of new company formation.

The MIT Entrepreneurship Program since its founding in 1990 has created classes taught by discipline-based academics and experienced, successful entrepreneurs, and venture capitalists, which have generated an effective blend for learning both theory and practice. Mixed-team project classes, consisting of both management students and engineers and scientists, have had great impact on MIT students in their understanding of the entrepreneurial process, have initiated their exposure to and engagement with new real-world enterprises, and have influenced the subsequent founding of many new companies. Cross-campus student-run activities such as the MIT $100 K Business Plan Competition have moved numerous students, often with faculty as team members, to develop their ideas to the point of public scrutiny. Participant teams in these student-run competitions have started more than 150 companies, many of them very successful.

The MIT Technology Licensing Office (TLO) has consistently been among the country's leading universities in licensing technology to start-up firms, licensing 210 new companies in the past 10 years, and many more start-ups before then. The TLO has also brought its experience and knowledge into active engagement with MIT students, faculty, and alumni.

The creation of formal MIT institutions focused upon encouraging entrepreneurship has accelerated significantly during the past decade. In 2000, the Venture Mentoring Service was begun to help any MIT-related individual — student, staff, faculty, alumnus/a — who was contemplating a start-up. It has already seen over 152 companies formed by those it has counseled.

The Deshpande Center for Technological Innovation was initiated in 2002 to provide small research grants to faculty whose ideas seemed especially likely to be able to be commercialized. In its first eight years, the Deshpande Center has funded more than 80 faculty research projects. A total number of 23 spinout companies have already been formed from these projects, most of those aided by student teams from the related Innovation Teams course, carried out jointly by Deshpande and the MIT Entrepreneurship Center.

In 2006, the MIT Sloan School of Management created a new Entrepreneurship & Innovation (E&I) "Track" within its MBA Program to provide intensive opportunities for those students who seem dedicated to an entrepreneurial life. It is too soon to know what eventual outcomes this focused approach will produce, but more than 40% of incoming MBA candidates are now enrolling in this concentration. Initial students have already engaged in numerous company-building activities and have won important university business plan competitions. The E&I track seems to have mobilized entrepreneurial efforts even by students not enrolled in the track, with 40 MBA graduates (12% of the class) founding new firms in 2010 rather than accepting employment in existing companies. This escalating focus on entrepreneurship has become evident even among the mid-career MIT Sloan Fellows and in the recently launched Executive MBA Program.

The 2007 founding of the Legatum Center for Development & Innovation has brought increased emphasis and resources for encouraging MIT students to found companies in low-income countries that would provide a bottoms-up approach to alleviating poverty and accelerating economic development. Legatum's fellowship program has led more students into participation in the $100 K Competition's Development Track and into formation of related club activities.

Beyond these MIT influences upon firm formation, 85% of the alumni entrepreneurs reported in the survey data that association with MIT had significantly helped their credibility with suppliers and customers. A total of 51% of the entrepreneurs also felt that their association with MIT helped in acquiring funding.

All of these forces — from initial orientation and culture to all encompassing clubs and activities to now-concentrated educational opportunities — contribute to building and sustaining the MIT entrepreneurial ecosystem, with extensive interactions across the Institute. That system has been uniquely productive in helping to create new firms that have had impressive economic impact.

2

The Role of MIT Alumni Companies in the US Economy

For some time, anecdotes and research have indicated significant entrepreneurial impact from MIT. In 2003, along with professional staff from MIT, the authors set about to attempt to quantify through surveys and research the actual economic impact of entrepreneurship among MIT alumni.[1] The results presented in this report — the first disclosure of our research results in regard to economic impact[2] — are supplemented with some detail on the history, institutions and culture that have combined to influence entrepreneurship at and from MIT.

In 2001, MIT sent a survey to all 105,928 living alumni with addresses on record. MIT received 43,668 responses from alumni. Of these, 34,846 answered the question about whether or not they had been entrepreneurs. A total of 8179 individuals (23.5% of the respondents) indicated that they had founded at least one company. In 2003, we developed and sent a survey instrument focused on the formation

---

[1] As indicated previously, "alumni" are defined by the MIT Alumni/ae Association to include all persons who received an "earned" degree from MIT, as well as those who were registered in a degree-granting program for at least one full undergraduate term or two full graduate terms.

[2] The initial version of this report was published in February 2009 by the Kauffman Foundation.

and operation of their firms to the 8044 entrepreneur respondents for whom we had complete addresses. Of this group, 2111 founders completed surveys. The database reported in this report was created from these surveys, as well as additional detailed analyses, including verification and updating of revenue and employment figures from the 2006 records of Compustat (public companies) and Dun & Bradstreet (private companies). The Appendix provides further details on the survey and estimation methods, some additional comparative statistics, as well as information on alumni entrepreneurship surveys carried out at several other universities.

Based on our extensive data collection and analyses, we conclude that, if the active companies founded by living MIT graduates formed an independent nation, conservative estimates indicate that their revenues would make that nation at least the 17th largest economy in the world. A less-conservative direct extrapolation of the underlying survey data boosts the numbers to some 33,600 total companies founded over the years by living MIT alumni, of which 25,800 (76%) still existed in 2006, employing 3.3 million people and generating annual worldwide revenues of nearly $2 trillion, the equivalent of the 11th-largest economy in the world.

For conservatism of our projections, we deliberately excluded from the database companies in which the MIT alumnus founder had already died prior to the survey, even if the company still survived, such as Hewlett-Packard or Intel. Even if the founder was still alive, we excluded from our database those MIT alumni-founded companies that had merged with or been sold to other firms prior to 2003, such as DEC, which had peak employment of 140,000 people prior to its merger with Compaq in 1998 (which later merged with Hewlett-Packard). Nor do the numbers include MIT alumni-founded firms that had closed prior to our original 2003 survey. These estimates similarly ignore all companies founded by non-alumni MIT faculty or staff. In addition, we do not examine the impact of MIT-generated science and technology on the overall innovation and competitiveness of government and industry beyond alumni-founded firms. Clearly, entrepreneurship likely has benefited from additional spillovers from the scientific and non-scientific advances emerging from MIT, its faculty, staff, and graduates.

Table 2.1. Estimated employment and sales data for all active MIT alumni companies.

Jobs	Percent of companies	Median employees	Median sales ($ millions)	Estimated total employees	Estimated total sales ($ millions)
More than 10,000	0.3	15,000	1523	1,339,361	1,389,075
1000–10,000	1.8	1927	308	1,043,932	235,532
Less than 1000	97.9	39	<1	900,001	226,671
Total	100.0	155	<1	3,283,294	1,851,278

Thus, we attempt to portray only an aspect of MIT's entrepreneurial impact.

As shown in Table 2.1, relatively few but larger companies account for a substantial proportion of the total sales and employment of all active MIT alumni-founded companies. We estimate in Table 2.1 that the 541 largest current MIT alumni companies (about 2% of the total estimated companies) — those with employment of 1000 or more — account for 88% of total sales and 83% of total employment of all the MIT alumni-founded firms. Most of these larger firms are quite old. However, many young graduates have managed to build their companies to impressive size in a short period of time. We estimate that 213 companies with a founder who graduated in the past 30 years (and 15 with founders who graduated in the past 15 years) have 500 or more employees. Of these 213 younger-but-larger companies, about 8% are in software, 10% in telecommunications, and 21% in electronics. Of the approximately 14,700 firms founded by MIT graduates from the past 15 years, 10% have already 100 or more employees. This is compared with 12% for founders out 15–30 years, and 13% for founders out 30–50 years.

Companies founded by MIT alumni have a broad footprint on the United States (and the globe). While more than a quarter of these active companies (projected to be 6900) have headquarters in Massachusetts, nearly 60% of the MIT alumni companies are located outside the Northeastern area of the United States. These companies have a major presence in the San Francisco Bay Area (Silicon Valley), southern California, the Washington–Baltimore–Philadelphia belt, the Pacific Northwest, the Chicago area, southern Florida, Dallas and Houston, and the industrial cities of Ohio, Michigan, and Pennsylvania.

2.1   Influence of Technology on Economic Impact

Among all of the companies founded by MIT alumni, technology has played very different roles in the formation and growth of the firms. At one extreme, the company may have been based upon a technological breakthrough, perhaps generated at a university research laboratory, without which there would have been no company. At the other extreme, such as in a management consulting firm or an architectural practice or a retail or distribution company, technology may have had no apparent role in influencing the founder(s)' decision and ability to start a firm. We attempt here to categorize the technological bases of the estimated 25,800 companies, still active in 2006 and founded by living MIT alumni. We know that MIT itself licenses technology to about 25 new start-ups each year, a critical base in their formation (see Section 4.3). However, it is clear that university-related technology, other than from licenses alone, has been influential in helping to establish the bases of most of these 25,800 firms. In fact, given that MIT alumni found about 900 or more companies per year, our overall assessment is that the broad education provided by the university is the dominant base from which graduates eventually transfer their new scientific and technological knowledge and skills to the marketplace. It is important to note that a large fraction of the MIT alumni entrepreneurs whom we have studied here have also received degrees from other universities, in the United States and other countries. Furthermore, a large fraction of the companies founded by MIT alumni have co-founders who may have been educated at still other institutions, so the population of universities that influence this technology flow is widespread.

Our survey database permits us to identify when a new firm's technology (1) was licensed directly from a university (MIT or elsewhere); or (2) came from a founder's thesis work or from his or her university lab or coursework, or the original product or service idea came from university research. (3) A faculty member might have been a company co-founder, or involved as a formal or informal advisor in the start-up. (4) Or the founding team may have met while working as students or staff in a university lab. If any one or more of these four general conditions were true in the company founding, we identify the firm's founding technology as "University-based."[3] If the company was started with some key technological knowledge or capability, but not derived from any of the listed university sources, we identify the firm as based on "Non-University Technology." That technology may have derived from work done by one or more of the founders in a company or government organization, but not at a university. The remaining companies are labeled as having "No Technology" base, including lacking any formal intellectual property or research and development efforts.

Table 2.2 presents the economic impact information displayed in Table 2.1, by size of firms, but now divided among the three clusters of "University Technology," "Non-University Technology," and "No Technology" base. The evidence is clear. Among at least the MIT alumni-founded firms, the principal economic impact is produced by those companies that were based in general upon university-derived technology. That group of firms alone employs 1.7 million of the total 3.3 million people worldwide, generating one trillion dollars of the $1.8 trillion in total global revenues coming from all of the MIT alumni-created companies. (By the way, more than half of those jobs were in the companies that relied primarily upon MIT technology, not technology from other universities.) The other companies that are technology-based, but from

Table 2.2. Estimated employment and sales data for all active MIT alumni companies, as influenced by technological base.

Jobs	Percent of companies	University Technology		Non-University Technology		No Technology	
		Estimated total employees	Estimated total sales ($ millions)	Estimated total employees	Estimated total sales ($ millions)	Estimated total employees	Estimated total sales ($ millions)
More than 10,000	0.3	610,770	$ 799,263	482,198	$ 480,475	246,393	$ 109,337
1000– 10,000	1.8	780,403	142,501	88,846	53,644	174,683	39,387
Less than 1000	97.9	325,744	56,840	514,188	161,823	60,069	8008
Total	100.0	1,716,917	$ 998,604	1,085,232	$ 695,942	481,145	$ 156,732

---

[3] Multiple aspects of these technology measures frequently apply simultaneously. For example, at least one of the other three university technology utilization criteria applies to all those founders who met in a university lab.

industry or government experiences or exposures, produce nearly 1.1 million jobs and $700 billion in sales. Together, the companies based upon technology account for 85% of all of the jobs and nearly 92% of the overall revenues produced by the "living" MIT alumni-founded firms. The non-technology-based companies indeed employ a not-insignificant almost half-million jobs; however, they are merely 15% of the economic consequences arising from the MIT alumni entrepreneurs. These data provide remarkable testimony to the economic impact of technology-based entrepreneurship. We suspect that similar results would derive from the entrepreneurial alumni of other universities that are strong in science and technology.

2.2   Additional Trends over the Decades

2.2.1   Growth in Numbers

We estimate that 2900 currently active companies were founded during the 1980s and as many as 9950 companies were founded during the 1990s, of which 5900 are still active. More than 5800 companies were created between 2000 and 2006. For each decade (using our linear projections from our database), Figure 2.1 shows the estimated yearly growth over the past 50 years of "first firms" founded by all MIT alumni. (We have no information on alumni company formation after 2006.) *New company formation by MIT graduates is accelerating.* (We omit from this figure but will later present our evidence on the second, third, and more companies generated by many of the MIT alumni over their entrepreneurial careers.)

Further evidence on the acceleration of MIT alumni entrepreneurship through the past five decades is obvious in Figure 2.2, where we limit ourselves for consistency to just the bachelor's degree recipients who responded to the 2003 survey of MIT alumni. The figure shows clearly that the cohort of bachelor's degree graduates from each successive decade has been forming more new first companies.[4]

---

[4] The MIT undergraduate class grew from about 900 per year in the 1950s to about 1050 in subsequent decades. Graduate school enrollments have grown considerably over the same time period, including, in particular, the growth of management graduate students that followed the formation of the MIT Sloan School of Management in 1952. In many of our

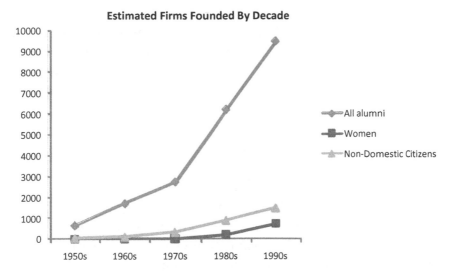

Fig. 2.1 Estimated number of "first-time" firms founded each decade by MIT alumni.

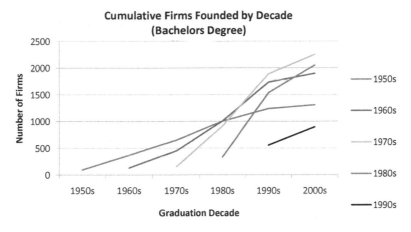

Fig. 2.2 Cumulative number of "first firms" founded by each decade's cohort of alumni (from limited sample only).

Two-thirds of the MIT alumni companies over the entire 60-years span of our data have been co-founded, with the size of the founding team steadily increasing from 2.3 in the 1950s to 3.3 in the 2000s.

analyses, we took these size changes into account via normalization per 1000 alumni at each decade. However, these normalized analyses did not alter any of the underlying trends reported here.

We also have found consistency over all these years in the attributed sources of the ideas for initiating these new enterprises. On average, two-thirds of the founders claim that the specific idea to start a firm came from experiences at work, about 15% from networking activities, and about 10% from research, albeit as indicated in Table 2.2 the technology base of the firms more frequently depends upon their university backgrounds.

2.2.2   More Diverse Entrepreneurs

We find evidence of significant shifts in some demographic characteristics among MIT entrepreneurs, particularly in gender and citizenship. The numerical growth of women entrepreneurs appears to mirror the growth in number of women graduating from all levels at MIT, rising from just over 10 female graduates per year (1%) in the 1930s to 43% of undergraduates and 30% of the graduate student population in 2006. Women alumnae lag their male classmates (but slowly are moving upward) in the proportion that become entrepreneurs. Women founders start appearing in the 1950s and, as shown in Figure 2.1, grow to 6% of the reporting sample by the 1990s, and are up to 10% by the 2000s.

Alumni who were not US citizens when admitted to MIT founded companies at different (usually higher per capita) rates relative to their American counterparts, with at least as many remaining in the United States to form their companies as are returning to their home countries. Figure 2.1 indicates that non-US citizens begin slight visibility as entrepreneurs in the 1940s, grow steadily to 12% of the new firm formations during the decade of the 1990s, and up to 17% by the 2000s.

About 30% of the foreign students who attend MIT found companies at some point in their lives. This is a much higher rate than for US citizens who attend MIT. We assume (but do not have data that might support this) that foreign students are more inclined from the outset to become entrepreneurs, as they had to seek out and get admitted to a foreign university, taking on the added risks of leaving their families and their home countries to study abroad. (MIT has only one campus in Cambridge, Mass., and, despite collaborations in many

Table 2.3. Estimated number of companies
founded by MIT "foreign-student" alumni.

Location of companies	Total	Manufacturing
United States	2340	673
Europe	790	51
Latin America	495	63
Asia	342	43

countries, does not operate any degree program outside of the United
States.) We estimate that about 5000 firms were started by MIT graduates who were not US citizens when they were admitted to MIT. *Half
of those companies created by "imported" entrepreneurs, 2340 firms,
are headquartered in the United States, generating their principal revenue ($16 billion) and employment (101,500 people) benefits here.* As
shown in Table 2.3, an even higher fraction of the manufacturing firms
founded by foreign students, which usually have far greater economic
impact than service companies, is located in the United States. The
largest non-US locations of foreign-alumni firms are in Europe and
Latin America. More than 775 MIT foreign-alumni businesses are in
Europe, most of which are in software and consulting. The greatest
numbers of these firms are in England, France, and Germany. Latin
America has an estimated 500 firms, most of which are in Mexico,
Brazil, and Venezuela. Asia has 342 firms of which the largest numbers
are in China, Japan, and India. However, we expect the Asian number
to grow rapidly as the Asian fraction of MIT foreign students continues
to grow, and as more of them return home.

As is true of all the alumni-founded firms, many of those started by
foreign students are sizable businesses but most are small; the median
number of employees of the MIT alumni companies in Europe and Asia
is 18 employees and the median revenues are a little more than $1 mil-
lion. Almost three-quarters of these businesses are started by alumni
with MIT graduate degrees; not too surprising, as historically MIT has
had few undergraduates from outside of the United States. (Additional
undergraduates had been born abroad, but were US citizens by the
time they entered MIT.) About half of the American founders have
advanced degrees from MIT.

Of the US-located companies founded by MIT's foreign students, 66% were started in the 1990s or 2000s. European alumni started 36% of the 2340 US-located firms and alumni from Asian countries started 28% of them. This geographic source distribution of US-located foreign alumni entrepreneurs will no doubt shift as Asians become a larger fraction of the MIT foreign-student population.

2.2.3   Case Example: Three Asian Entrepreneurs — Patni, Huang, and Zhang

Over the past 50 years, most MIT foreign-student alumni entrepreneurs have come from Europe. However, the dramatic rise during the 1980s and 1990s of Asian graduate students in all MIT departments has produced important growth of Asian entrepreneurs. Here are three brief success stories, all linked to computers and the Internet. All three received their undergraduate education abroad, and then came to MIT for graduate study. One stayed in the United States to create and build his company, another went back to his homeland, and the third divided his time and company between the US and his home country, establishing a global firm that operated worldwide.

2.2.3.1   Naren Patni, MIT, 1969

Narendra Patni, a bachelor's degree graduate of the Indian Institute of Technology, came to MIT on a fellowship to study electrical engineering. In 1969, Naren received two MIT master's degrees, in EE and management. Intrigued by the growing opportunities in computers and information technology, he decided to stay in Cambridge, working part-time for Professor Jay Forrester (MIT, 1945), himself a computer pioneer, while joining with his brothers in India to start one of the earliest software "outsourcing" companies. Naren sold projects in the United States, and his brothers managed the software developers in India. Patni Computer Systems Limited was incorporated formally in 1978, a number of years after the brothers actually began to work together to build a business. While Patni Computer Systems was primarily in software, for several years the company moved into hardware too, first by becoming the Indian distributor for Data General computers, and then by importing computer components and subsystems for assembly and sales in India.

Returning to software development and support and related services, Patni Computer Systems grew through highly volatile periods to eventual global revenues in 2010 of US $700 million, net income of $33 million, and 17,500 employees in offices across the Americas, Europe, and Asia-Pacific. For many years, Patni (the person and the company) operated out of dual headquarters in Cambridge, MA (across the street from the MIT Sloan School) and Mumbai, India. From its modest beginnings, the firm rose to being traded on both the Bombay Stock Exchange and the New York Stock Exchange. In January 2011, iGate Corporation announced that it had reached an agreement to purchase 63% of the company from major stockholders and that it would offer to purchase up to 20% more shares in the open market.[5]

2.2.3.2   Robert Huang, MIT, 1979

Robert Huang, a native of Taiwan, spent much of his youth in Japan, including receiving his bachelor's degree from Kyushu University. Following advanced degrees from the University of Rochester and his master's degree from MIT Sloan, Bob moved to California to become Headquarters Sales Manager for Advanced Micro Devices. Within one year, in 1980, Huang left AMD to establish COMPAC Corporation as a distributor of computers and related IT equipment, in time changing its name to Synnex Corporation. For almost 30 years Bob served as President and Co-Chief Executive, and then as Chairman of the Board, of Synnex.

During those 30 years, Synnex has had a superb record of growth of revenues and employees. It went public in 2003 on the New York Stock Exchange and has continued to broaden its base in the electronics and computer industries. In 2010, it generated overall revenues of $8.6 billions, up nearly one billion dollars from 2009. Its approximately 8000 employees are worldwide, but with most of them in the United States.

---

[5] http://en.wikipedia.org/wiki/Patni_Computer_Systems#Acquisition_By_iGate_Corporation, accessed on March 5, 2011.

2.2.3.3   Charles Zhang, MIT, 1994

In spring 1996, Charles Zhang poked his head into the MIT Sloan office of Professor Edward Roberts (MIT, 1957), and asked if he might come in for a brief chat. He had received his undergraduate education in Beijing at Tsinghua University, the so-called "MIT of China," and then won a competitive fellowship to come to MIT. During the brief period since receiving his MIT PhD in experimental physics, Charles had been working part-time for the MIT Industrial Liaison Program, leading various Chinese visitors to meetings with MIT faculty and labs. Charles' quick and somewhat shocking response to Professor Roberts' welcoming inquiry was "I want to go home to China and start an Internet company."

After three months of probing, planning, searching for focus while also seeking funds, Zhang and Roberts incorporated Internet Technologies China, Inc. (ITC) in August 1996. With $225,000 raised from three MIT-related investors, most of it left on deposit in the Bank of Boston, Charles returned to Beijing to attempt his pioneering start-up. The next two years were formidable for Zhang and his co-founder, establishing China's first Internet portal in a setting of a not-yet-existing market, unclear and conflicting government rules and regulations, a wholly inexperienced CEO, and little surrounding infrastructure for accessing professional or managerial help. In 1998, ITC finally closed on its initial serious financing, led by Intel Capital and Morningstar Group from Hong Kong, in time to launch its Yahoo-like search engine, named "Sohu," Chinese for "search fox," a smart and quick animal ☺. Changing its corporate name to match its search product, Sohu.com began its volatile climb in sales, employees, multiple products, and eventually profitability.

Now public on NASDAQ since July 2000, Sohu.com, Inc. has become one of China's largest Internet firms. It partially spun out its gaming division, Changyou, in a NASDAQ IPO in April 2009. The Sohu Group completed its 2010 fiscal year with US $612 million in revenues, $198 million in profits, and about 5200 total employees. Zhang is still the CEO, and Roberts is the only remaining non-Chinese Board member.

2.2.4   Younger Entrepreneurs

The tendencies shown in Figures 2.1–2.4 are clear: *More entrepreneurs emerge out of each successive MIT graduating class, and they start their first companies sooner and at earlier ages.* To illustrate this, in Figure 2.3 we display for bachelor's degree graduates how many companies were founded by each decade's cohort group as a function of the number of years following their MIT graduation. During each successive decade, the cohort of graduating alumni got started in its entrepreneurial behavior sooner (i.e., the cumulative number of companies rises much faster in terms of years after graduation) than the preceding decade's cohort.

Figure 2.4 shows three frequency distributions of the ages of MIT alumni first-time entrepreneurs for firms founded during and prior to the 1970s, for those founded in the 1980s, and for those founded in the 1990s. Note the general shifts in the three curves over the years. The distributions show that the more recent entrepreneurs include many more

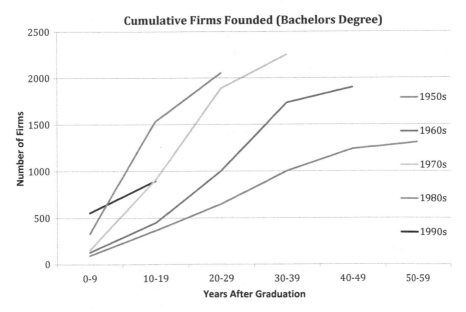

Fig. 2.3 Firms founded by years after graduation for each decade's cohort of alumni (from limited sample only).

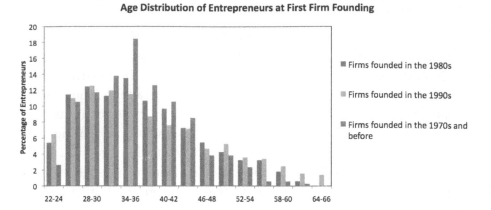

Fig. 2.4 Age distributions of entrepreneurs at time of "first firm" founding.

from the younger age brackets, as well as slightly more from the late 40s and 50s age brackets. During and prior to the 1970s, 24% of the first-time entrepreneurs were under 30 years of age; during the 1980s that number grew to 31%; in the 1990s, 36% of the founders were under 30. During and prior to the 1970s, 30% of the first-time founders were older than 40 years of age; during the 1980s, 28% were older than 40; and in the 1990s, 35% were older than 40. More than half of all MIT alumni companies now (meaning as of the 2006 data collection) are founded within 10 years of the time the founder graduates from MIT; one-quarter of the companies are founded within six years after graduation.

Anecdotally, about 12% (40 students) of the 2010 MIT Sloan School's graduating MBAs started new firms prior to or at the time of their graduation, suggesting that this trend is continuing and perhaps accelerating. The median age of first-time entrepreneurs gradually has declined from about age 40 (1950s) to about age 30 (1990s). Correspondingly, the average time lag between graduation and first-firm founding for alumni from the more recent decades has dropped to as low as four years from graduation during the "Internet bubble" years of the 1990s, but this downward leap is an anomaly.

To check on possible special industry effects, we separated out those who had formed software companies. Figure 2.5 shows that the majority of software founders over the entire 50 years period of our study are age

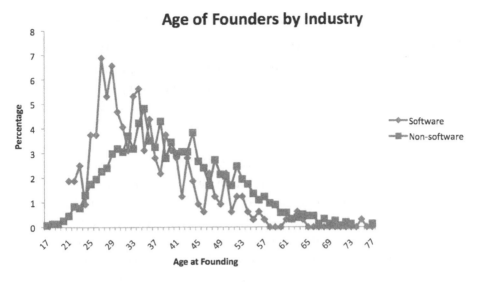

Fig. 2.5 Age of founders: Software vs other industries.

Table 2.4. Median age of "first firm" founders, by decade of graduation.

First Firm Founders	1950s	1960s	1970s	1980s	1990s
All	40.5	39.0	35.0	32.0	28.0
Non-US Citizens	38.0	35.5	36.5	32.0	29.0
Women	42.0	41.0	40.0	35.0	29.0

30 or younger, and the majority of non-software industry founders are below age 35 the year they found their first firms. However, not shown in this report, the increase in software entrepreneurship in recent years does not account statistically for the continuing decline in the average entrepreneurial age at the time of first company formation.

We support the above arguments with the data in Table 2.4, demonstrating that the ages of first-time MIT alumni entrepreneurs have been getting younger each decade, whether male or female, US or foreign citizen. (The big drop in the 1990s reflects the fact that many more graduates from the 1990s will form companies later, which will then move that average age upward to some extent. Technically, we identify this phenomenon as a situation of "right-side censoring" of the data, and correct for it in all of our statistical analyses.)

2.2.5   Case Example: Harmonix Music Systems[6]

What do Facebook and Harmonix have in common? Both start-ups were founded by very young entrepreneurs, aiming primarily at young people who want to communicate with each other. For Facebook, at age 20, Mark Zuckerberg's media were words and photos. For Harmonix, the medium for Alex Rigopulos (age 24) and Eran Egozy (age 22) was music.

Rigopulos (MIT, 1992) and Egozy (MIT, 1995) were both musicians, studying computers, engineering, and music at MIT, and working at the MIT Media Lab. They founded Harmonix Music Systems in 1995 so "non-musicians... [could] experience the sheer joy of music creation — normally something only afforded to accomplished musicians."[7] They raised about $100,000 from friends and family to start the company, and then had nearly zero revenues during the first five years! Indeed, they had entered the MIT $10K business plan competition (described in depth later in this report) and didn't get past Phase 1 of the competition. Despite essentially creating the category of music video games and attracting numerous industry awards, Harmonix generated some revenues but continued to fail commercially through 2004. Harmonix stayed alive through this long period with additional "raises" of funds, the Series B round led by Brad Feld (MIT, 1987), a successful software entrepreneur who later became quite prominent as a venture capitalist and seed stage investor.

In 2005, the company created "Guitar Hero," using a guitar-shaped controller. That product took off, resulting in their also successful "Guitar Hero II" in 2006. Activision quickly acquired the rights to "Guitar Hero" and has published later versions on its own. In response, MTV (then part of Viacom) bought Harmonix for $175 million upfront plus an "earn-out bonus" based on their products' future sales, which generated $150 million in later payments to all the Harmonix shareholders.

---

[6] Some of the information here comes from an interview with Eran Egozy on March 10, 2011.

[7] http://www.techstars.org/mentors/eegozy/, accessed on March 6, 2011.

Harmonix released "Rock Band" in November 2007, "Rock Band II" in 2008, and "The Beatles: Rock Band" in 2009, and over several years produced a massive and continuing number of downloadable songs for various platforms (such as PlayStation, Wii, and Xbox).

In December 2010, Viacom announced that it had sold Harmonix to Harmonix-SBE Holdings LLC, a group that includes the company's original two co-founders and its previous investors. Alex and Eran are back running their music show in Cambridge, now with about 200 employees. Their latest release is "Dance Central," exclusively for Microsoft's Kinect for the X-Box, which continues the Harmonix history of innovation in the world of music.

2.2.6   Serial Entrepreneurs

To this point, we have focused primarily on the vast number of MIT alumni who have founded their first enterprises. Yet the phenomenon of MIT graduates embarking on careers of repeat or "serial" entrepreneurship appears to be growing over time. Using only the limited data from the 2003 survey, without any scaling adjustment, Figure 2.6 shows the number of first firms, second firms, and third (and more) firms by their founding year. By definition, "first-time" firms are the most prevalent, and the number of first firms founded increases over the years. Separate from any other trends, we expect this increase due to the fact that each year adds another year of graduates with the potential for entering entrepreneurship.

Table 2.5 presents, by their decade of graduation, the number of entrepreneurs founding one firm up to five or more firms. The high in the database is 11 firms founded by one alumnus up to 2003. (However, we are now aware of at least one MIT alumnus who has doubled that number as of 2011! In its brief founder biography for Dr. Robert Langer (MIT, 1974), the Pulmatrix, Inc. web site indicates that Langer is a founder of over 20 successful companies, including Momenta, Alnylam, Transform Pharmaceuticals, Pervasis, and Advanced Inhalation Research.[8]) As listed in Table 2.5, "Percent Repeat," is the percentage of founders from each decade of MIT graduates who have started more

---

[8] http://www.pulmatrix.com/about-founders.html#, accessed on March 24, 2011.

Year of Founding

Fig. 2.6 Histogram of repeat founders among MIT alumni entrepreneurs (from limited sample only).

Table 2.5.   One-time and repeat MIT founders by decade of graduation (percent).

Total number of firms founded	Decade							
	1930s	1940s	1950s	1960s	1970s	1980s	1990s	2000s
1	67%	61%	56%	54%	48%	57%	61%	59%
2	0	11	21	20	23	22	23	28
3	0	9	10	11	16	11	9	9
4	11	8	7	7	6	5	3	3
5+	22	11	7	9	7	5	4	0
Percent repeat	33%	39%	44%	46%	52%	43%	39%	41%

than one firm. Across the decades, MIT alumni founders who have founded multiple start-ups have grown from 33% of those who graduated in the 1930s to 52% of those who graduated in the 1970s.[9] The decrease in Table 2.5 entry percentage from the 1980s on is due to the

---

[9] This statistic uses the total number of firms each entrepreneur claimed to have started. For the remainder of the analyses, we use the number of firms for which they listed the company names and founding dates in the 2003 survey. The listings are more reliable and conservative but were capped by the survey instrument at five.

fact that many of the more recent graduates have not yet had time to start a second (or more) firm but certainly may do so in the future.

The MIT alumni entrepreneurs who eventually found multiple companies differ substantially from "single-firm-only" entrepreneurs, and their companies are quite different too. For example, proportionately more of the repeat founders are not US citizens and a slightly higher proportion of the repeat entrepreneurs hold master's degrees. Relative to the repeat entrepreneurs, those who found only one company throughout their lives are older when they establish their sole company and have a longer lag from graduation to that founding. Repeat/serial entrepreneurs enter entrepreneurship much sooner, which likely reflects their own strong entrepreneurial tendencies while also giving them more time to start subsequent firms.

Table 2.6, directly from our limited 2003 sample, contains economic impact indicators of the one-time and repeat entrepreneurs in terms of firms founded, revenues, and employees. The representative MIT alumni entrepreneur founds 2.07 companies over his lifetime. However, the difference is that the one-time-only entrepreneur founds just one company, and the average serial entrepreneur founds 3.25 firms. As shown in Table 2.6 repeat entrepreneurs have a substantial economic impact relative to the percentage of total entrepreneurs, accounting for about three times the total company revenues and employees as the single-firm founders. *Thus, a third observed trend is that, over time, the number of multiple companies founded per MIT entrepreneurial*

Table 2.6.   Economic impact of one-time and repeat entrepreneurs (from limited sample only).

Category of entrepreneur	One-time entrepreneurs	Repeat/serial entrepreneurs
Total sales (in '000 $2006)	$9,876,900	$29,190,000
Total employment (2006)	111,915	344,208
Total No. of firms founded	1086	3193
Total founders in the sample	1086	981
Percentage of entrepreneurs	52.5	47.5
Percentage of firms	25.4	74.6
Percentage of total revenues	25.3	74.7
Percentage of total employment	24.5	75.5

alumnus has been increasing, with dramatically increased economic impact per graduate.

2.2.7   Case Example: Always an Entrepreneur — Diane Greene, MIT, 1978

> "It's what I love!" Diane exclaimed as she sat down to tell her story of entrepreneurship. Being an entrepreneur came naturally to this MIT alumna. "Ever since I was a child, I always loved starting new things."

While at MIT, her downstairs neighbors in Central Square, Cambridge, a group of MIT grad students studying artificial intelligence with Professor Seymour Papert, had a significant impact on her future career and entrepreneurial endeavors. They became her model for the type of very smart, highly engaged persons with whom she wanted to work in founding firms. "VMware," despite being in the heart of Silicon Valley, she told me, "was full of MIT people."

After MIT, Diane moved to California and soon to Hawaii, where she began to work with the group that was creating the sport of windsurfing. She helped start the San Francisco Classic and was the first woman to win that windsurfing competition. She's an avid sailor and ran engineering for Windsurfing International. After a second master's degree at UC Berkeley, she went to work for Sybase and then moved to Tandem. She held technical leadership positions there and at Silicon Graphics, before co-founding VXtreme in 1995 to develop and market a complete software solution for high-quality business video over the Internet. Diane sold VXtreme to Microsoft for $75 million. In 1997, Greene was working on her second start-up, a software company later bought by CMGI. She said that the decision to become an entrepreneur came naturally because she felt that she had been an entrepreneur within every organization she ever worked.

Diane took some time off after that acquisition and began her family, but was quickly back to entrepreneurship again. Along with her husband, Mendel Rosenblum, and three other Stanford co-founders, she created VMware in 1998 and became its CEO. Diane had also helped to fund the effort with her proceeds from the VXtreme acquisition. Her attitude has always been that she can make anything successful, if you just navigate and problem-solve relentlessly until you find a way to a successful outcome. Diane and her co-founders built the virtualization market and she led the business to a $1.9 billion run rate with 53% year-on-year growth in her last full quarter there.

Now, rather than resting on her accomplishments, as a true serial entrepreneur Diane is looking around for her next big entrepreneurial project to undertake.

2.2.8   MIT Founders and MIT Course Majors

More MIT founders, over 20% of the total, come from the Institute's electrical engineering and computer science programs (the two are linked in the same MIT department), than from any other department. Other programs heavily represented among the founders are: management; mechanical, chemical, and civil engineering; architecture; physics; and aeronautics.

Over the years, an interesting shift has occurred, reflecting an underlying change at MIT in the course majors taken by company founders. More than 65% of the founders who graduated more than 50 years ago were engineering majors. Only 44% of company founders who graduated in the last 15 years are engineers, whereas 32% are from the social sciences/management departments. We estimate the total number of MIT alumni companies founded (but not all of them still in business independently) by living engineering majors as 17,090, compared with 9100 companies founded by science majors, and 6860 companies by management majors, certainly affected by the relative sizes of the graduating populations.

Some correlation, but no predictable connection, exists between the founder's MIT major and the type of company. For example, life-science graduates found only 10% of alumni-created biotech and medical companies; 59% of the biotech and medical start-ups are founded by engineers. Social science and management graduates account for 9% of electronics firms, 10% of other manufacturing firms, and 20% of software companies, whereas engineering graduates account for 46% of the companies in finance and start 45% of the management consulting firms. These differences reflect, in part, the additional degrees of the MIT alumni, whether from MIT or from other universities, and/or the backgrounds of their co-founders.

We normalized the number of entrepreneurs from each of the five MIT Schools by using the numbers graduating in each decade as our bases for normalization. Despite increased participation over time from science graduates, the percentage of them who became entrepreneurs is still the smallest of all study areas, over essentially the entire period of time studied. The data show that, proportionately, from 50 to 100% more MIT engineering graduates than science alumni have eventually become entrepreneurs. Management graduates overall seem to be at least as inclined proportionately to become entrepreneurs as MIT engineering graduates. Architecture alumni are, on a proportional basis, perhaps surprisingly, the most likely among graduates of all the MIT schools to strike out on their own. However, this no doubt reflects a dominant "industry" structure of large numbers of small architectural practices, with relatively frequent changes in partnerships (i.e., new "firms").

Table 2.7 provides further details on the trends in three selected academic areas of MIT: electrical engineering and computer science (EECS), biology/life sciences, and management. EECS has, by tradition, been the largest MIT department and the most evident home of its entrepreneurial offshoots. Biology/life sciences is an up-and-coming "technology change area," including several MIT departments, and we wish to portray its entrepreneurial inclinations. Management education appears to have established itself as a common ground for entrepreneurial interest development and we want to examine how deeply rooted are these indicators.

Table 2.7. Proportion of founders from three selected academic areas of MIT (percent of all MIT alumni companies founded during the decade).

"First firm" founders	1950s	1960s	1970s	1980s	1990s
EE & CS degrees	20.4	26.5	18.7	25.4	22.7
Life Sciences degrees	0.0	2.7	4.0	4.9	4.7
Management degrees	16.7	14.3	13.5	13.8	15.8

The data show that the percentage of founders graduating with degrees in biology and/or the life sciences has indeed increased over the years, but appears to have leveled off in recent decades at around 5%. The percentage of founders who are EECS majors remains the highest at slightly more than 20% and those with management degrees hover around 15%. Both EECS and Management appear to be relatively stable in their proportionate supply of entrepreneurs over the decades.

2.2.9 Case Example: Meditech and Its Founders

When Ed Roberts (MIT, 1957) showed up at the Massachusetts General Hospital (MGH) Laboratory for Computer Medicine, he knew only that Neil Pappalardo (MIT, 1964) was a very smart guy who had developed the MUMPS programming language for medical software, and that Neil was strongly considering leaving MGH to start his own company. Roberts was several months along in his search for a local team with whom he might start a new medical software applications firm. His MIT undergraduate friend, Steve Lorch (MIT, 1959), had recommended Pappalardo as a good target. Neil introduced his lab "partners," Curt Marble (MIT, 1963), and Jerry Grossman (MIT, 1961). Neil, Curt, and Ed had all been undergraduates in Course 6, MIT Electrical Engineering, although the three of them were doing rather different things: Pappalardo was a key software developer, Marble worked primarily on hardware development with Neil, connecting various medical equipments to the computer via A/D converters, and Roberts was a professor at MIT Sloan, albeit working at that time on issues of healthcare management. Grossman was also an MIT undergrad alumnus, but had majored in Humanities & Science, with focus on pre-med, and then received his MD degree from the University of Pennsylvania. He was the interface between the Mass. General computer lab projects and the physicians in various parts of the hospital.

The two-hour initial meeting among these four MIT alumni was more like a loud debate society gathering than the congenial starting of a new enterprise. Neil talked about leaving to create a medical programming company, and Ed argued that you needed a base of software products to build a firm. Jerry helped by describing the several different applications that the lab had underway, such as patient medical history-taking, chemical laboratory automation, and patient enrollment and record-keeping. Despite the arguments, the group agreed to meet again in a week, and Roberts went home and placed his notes into a folder that he marked "Medical Systems Corporation." Over the next several months the four met repeatedly and progressed in their plans for a company launch, with Roberts developing the business plan and beginning the search for funding.

Discussions got very sensitive when Ed insisted that they needed to add a sales or marketing person to the group in order to have more than just great technology. Mort Ruderman, an alumnus of nearby Northeastern University, and the medical cross-products manager for DEC, was the only person the MGH team knew who fit the description of being knowledgeable in hospital sales/marketing. In time, Mort was persuaded to join this noisy group, which decided on the company name of Medical Information Technology (note the M, I, T initials) or Meditech for short. Mort became the start-up CEO and Neil the CTO, with Neil succeeding to the top position after the first few years. The company was founded in 1969 and funded immediately by EG&G, Inc.

Meditech has many unique characteristics, including that it has remained private and independent, despite many attempts by others to buy the company or take it public. It may well be the oldest independent software company in Massachusetts.[10] Over time, EG&G gradually sold all of its stock back to Meditech, so that now the company is owned almost entirely by its founders and later employees. It has grown very successfully, broadened its software systems coverage to all clinical, financial, and administrative aspects of hospital IT needs, and has the largest percentage market penetration (about 30%) of any hospital information systems company in the United States. For calendar 2010, Meditech had done $459 million in sales, made $109 million in profits after taxes, and ended up with 3300 employees. Pappalardo had just moved up from CEO to Chairman of the Board, Roberts and

---

[10] http://www.meditech.com/CorporateTimeline/homepage.htm.

Table 2.8.   MIT alumni companies by industry.

Industry	No. of Firms	Median employment	Median revenue ($000s)
Aerospace	467	15	1200
Architecture	1209	5	265
Biomedical	500	27	2000
Chemicals and materials	742	25	1275
Consumer products	1417	23	1500
Management consulting	2239	2	200
Electronics	3285	25	2000
Energy and utilities	789	8	508
Finance	1111	7	1800
Law and accounting	1046	8	450
Machinery	322	25	2600
Publishing and schools	564	12	1200
Software	5009	22	1500
Telecommunications	902	5	143
Other manufacturing	773	20	1600
Other services	5395	30	1750

Ruderman were still Board members, Marble had retired a few years before, and Grossman had unfortunately died.

2.2.10   Industry Composition and Effects

Table 2.8 shows an industry breakdown of MIT alumni companies by estimated number of firms, median employment, and median revenues. MIT alumni found companies in a diverse array of industries, although they do tend to cluster in certain sectors. About 3300 companies, employing an estimated total of 436,100 people, are in electronics, which (as used here loosely) includes computers, semi-conductors, instruments, telecommunications equipment, and electrical machinery and appliances. These electronics firms make up 13% of the total MIT alumni companies. All told, manufacturing firms make up 13% of the MIT alumni companies, 21% of total employment, and 6% of total sales.[11] In the United States as a whole, manufacturing accounts

---

[11] Not all electronics firms are in manufacturing. Some, for example, are in IC design (computer companies and telecommunications also were grouped with electronics). The estimate depends on how we calculate what is truly manufacturing. The Standard Industrial Classification codes (which are admittedly imperfect) of the companies indicate 13% with manufacturing codes. However, the entrepreneurs' industry self-reports suggest that

for less than 11% of total employment. Naturally, company size varies according by industry. Although their cumulative impact is significant, the median size in every industry is quite small, reflecting the overall national experience and the large number of young firms. However, the top 541 alumni companies have produced impressive results, as shown in Table 2.1.

Firms in software, electronics (including instruments, semiconductors, and computers), and biotech form a special subset of the MIT alumni companies. These high-technology firms (1) spend more of their revenues on research and development, (2) are more likely to hold one or more patents, and (3) tend to export a higher percentage of their products. They are more likely than companies in other industries to provide the bases for long-term economic growth. Together, firms in these three industries account for one-third of the employment in all MIT alumni companies; electronics, and instrument firms alone account for more than 13%.

The expansion plans of the companies we surveyed form an interesting "leading indicator," pointing to growth prospects by industry. More than 30% of the firms in chemicals, aerospace, and biotech are planning to expand. They are followed closely by telecommunications and by consumer products companies.

2.2.11   Global Markets

In any regional economy, firms that sell out-of-region play the major role in driving economic growth because, as these firms grow in total revenues (much of it not in the local area), they are also growing in local employment, and they create markets for utilities, service firms, retailers, and other local-market businesses. MIT alumni companies have a disproportionate importance to their local economies because so many of them are manufacturing, biotech, and software firms (48% of the employment of MIT alumni companies), which tend to compete in and sell to national and world markets. Overall, 54% of alumni company

---

manufacturing constitutes as much as 31%. The truth is probably between these two estimates at around 20%, much higher than for the United States as a whole, as we would expect for graduates of a science and technology-based university.

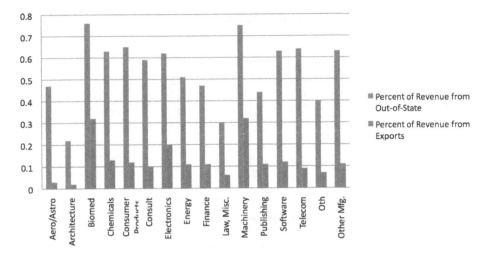

Fig. 2.7 Sales of MIT alumni companies out-of-state and exported abroad.

sales are to out-of-state markets; 13% of total sales come from goods or services sold by US firms abroad. Figure 2.7 shows these percentages by industry. For electronics, chemical, machinery, biotech, software, and management consulting firms, 65% of sales are out-of-state. The only industries whose companies have in-state sales amounting to 50% or more of total revenues are architects, finance companies, publishing, and law firms.

Across all industries, exports (outside of the United States by US-based firms) account for 13% of the sales revenues of MIT alumni companies. Exports are slightly higher for biomedical, machinery, and electronics firms (more than 20%). Companies in all other industries have an average export share of slightly less than 10%. These high-tech, high-growth industries clearly depend on foreign as well as domestic markets.

Figures 2.8 and 2.9 present the distributions by industry of the 2003 survey responses. Among manufacturing industries, electronics has held its own for six decades as a major opportunity area for MIT alumni entrepreneurs. On the services side, software firms have grown strikingly as a percentage of firms founded since the 1950s. Also of note is the rapid growth since the 1960s of ventures in financial services and management/financial consulting, no doubt reflecting both the market

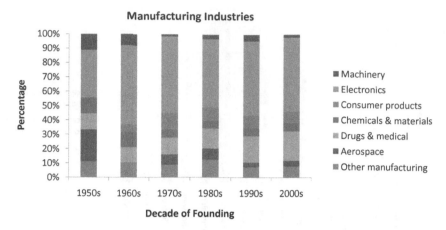

Fig. 2.8 Changing mix of manufacturing start-ups (percent).

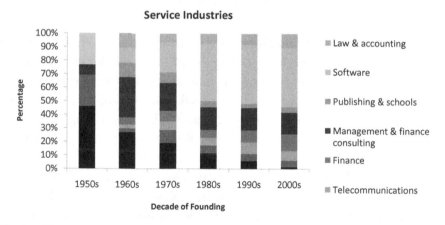

Fig. 2.9 Changing mix of services start-ups (percent).

opportunities and the increased number of MIT Sloan master's degree graduates during this period. Some of the trends may be attributable to changes in the size of certain departments relative to the rest of MIT (for example, architecture).

Figure 2.8 shows the trends over 60 years in the mix of new manufacturing companies being formed by MIT alumni, the dominance of electronics firms, and an increase in drugs and biomedical firms. Mirroring similar trends in the overall United States and world economies, the percentage of MIT alumni manufacturing firms has been

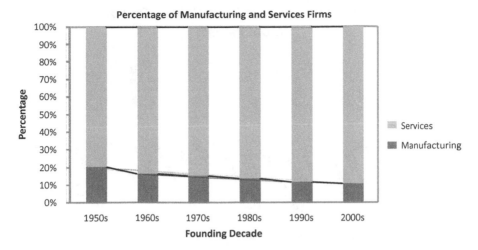

Fig. 2.10 Steady decline in manufacturing vs services start-ups (percent).

slowly decreasing over the decades, as shown in Figure 2.10. From a high of about 20% manufacturing firms in the 1950s, about 10% of the firms founded in the 1990s and 2000s were manufacturing firms. However, they employ about 30% of the total employees of all MIT alumni firms. An interesting observation from Table 2.3 shown earlier in this report is that the US-located companies founded by MIT foreign-student alumni include more than 28% in manufacturing. The overseas-located firms established by foreign alumni include fewer than 10% in manufacturing.

2.2.12 Patents and Research Expenditures

In all, between nearly 30% and more than 40% of the surveyed firms in aero/astro, biomed, chemicals, electronics, and machinery hold at least one patent. Consistent with their reputations as the two premier technology locations in the country, as shown in Figure 2.11, California and Massachusetts firms are more likely to hold patents than are their colleagues in the same industries in other states. The companies that hold patents average around 26 patents each.

Since larger companies are more likely to have had the time, technical, and legal resources, as well as business orientation, to generate and protect intellectual property portfolios, larger companies are more

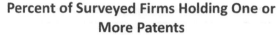

Percent of Surveyed Firms Holding One or More Patents

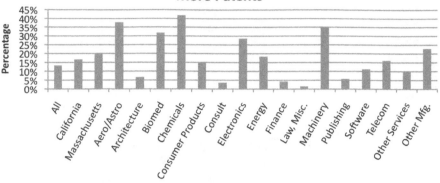

Fig. 2.11 Surveyed firms holding one or more patents (percent).

Spending on R&D and Marketing, MIT-Alumni Companies

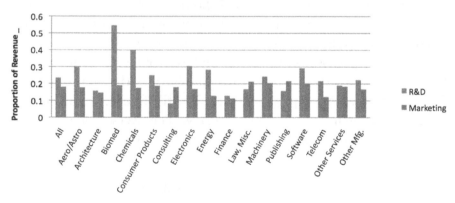

Fig. 2.12 Spending on R&D and marketing in MIT alumni companies.

likely to hold patents (59% of companies with 500 or more employees hold at least one patent, compared with only 16% of companies with fewer than 50 employees). The larger companies also hold more patents (64 per company for those with 500 or more employees vs. only 0.78 for those with fewer than 50 workers).

Aerospace, biotech, electronics, chemicals, and software firms tend to report spending more on R&D, as shown in Figure 2.12. The average for all surveyed MIT alumni companies is 24% of total revenues spent on research and development in 2006, whereas software companies spend 29%. In contrast, the average R&D spending for all US firms is estimated by the National Science Foundation to be 3.5% of sales in 2007, demonstrating rather dramatically the extraordinary scientific and technological base of the MIT alumni firms. Average MIT companies' spending on marketing is 18% of revenue.

2.2.13   Competitive Edge and Obstacles to Success

The recent survey of MIT alumni entrepreneurs has generated some interesting insights into these knowledge-based companies and what gives them a competitive advantage. The survey listed competitive factors and asked respondents to rank each of them in importance. The most frequently cited factors perceived as vital to competitive advantage were (1) superior performance, (2) customer service/responsiveness, (3) employee enthusiasm, (4) management expertise, and (5) innovation/new technology — all ahead of product price. Although price is not unimportant (it is hard for a company to compete if its price is unreasonable), if a start-up has a cutting-edge product with outstanding performance and good customer service, it can reasonably charge a premium.

In the aerospace industry (where government is the major client), price is the second-most important factor (behind superior performance). Price is least important to finance and consulting firms. Time to market is particularly important in electronics and instruments, software, and aerospace, and least important in management consulting and finance. Innovation, new technology, and time to market are particularly important to founders who graduated in the past 15 years.

A total of 85% of the alumni entrepreneurs reported association with MIT as having helped boost their credibility with suppliers and customers. A total of 51% of the entrepreneurs also felt that their association with MIT had helped in acquiring funding. Had we studied alumni entrepreneurs from Stanford University, Cal Tech or other research-intensive universities, we no doubt would have found similar linkages between entrepreneur credibility and the reputation of their alma mater.

Government regulation mattered most to aerospace, chemical, and energy firms, reflecting the role of the government in defense procurement, environmental regulation, and utility regulation. Government regulation made much less difference to software and publishing companies and to company founders who graduated in the past 15 years relative to their older counterparts.

2.2.14   Firm Location Decisions

Almost all founders (89%) started their companies in the general location in which they were living at the time. The largest fraction of these founders (65%) indicated that they were living there because this was where they had been employed, and 15% indicated that they were living there because that location was where they attended university, which often was MIT and, in other cases, another graduate school.

The earliest studies of MIT spin-off companies, those started by the former employees of MIT's Instrumentation Laboratory (in Cambridge) and MIT's Lincoln Laboratory (in Lexington and Concord MA, 15 miles from the MIT campus), carefully analyzed many factors, including where those companies were located geographically. Those from the Instrumentation Lab strongly clustered (90%) within one mile of the lab's MIT Cambridge buildings. Those from the Lincoln Laboratory were primarily in the nearby Boston suburbs, within a few miles of Lincoln Lab. No overlap occurred in the two circles that enveloped the locations of most of the two labs' spin-offs. When teams formed the basis of these companies (most cases), the strongest commonality the founders had with each other, beyond their technical skills and their shared entrepreneurial interests, was their prior commuting pattern. It appears that the latter dominated the location decisions ☺. This was reinforced by the fact that more than half of all new companies are formed on a part-time basis, whether coming from university departments or labs or from industrial firms. This "moonlighting" pattern of new company formation essentially requires that the new "part-time" start-up be quite close physically to the continuing full-time employer.

When asked what factors influenced the location of their companies, the most common responses (in order) were (1) where the founders

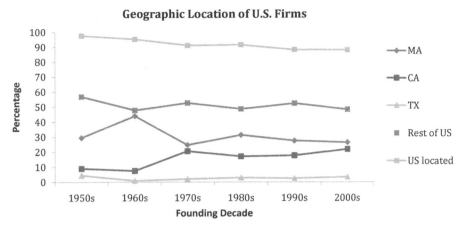

Fig. 2.13 Location of MIT alumni firms in the United States.

lived, (2) network of contacts, (3) quality of life, (4) proximity to major markets, and (5) access to skilled professional workers (engineers, technicians, and managers). Taxes and the regulatory environment were rated as less important factors for most industries. High-tech start-ups are highly dependent on the availability of skilled professionals to build reliable, high-quality, innovative products. The companies locate where these professionals like to live.

Within the United States, the development of Silicon Valley and other entrepreneurial locations in California is shown in Figure 2.13 by the shift over 50 years toward about 22% of MIT graduates starting their companies there, while still having about 26% locating in Massachusetts. We do not know how many of them attended graduate schools in California after receiving a bachelor's degree from MIT. New York and Texas are home to about 8% of the firms in total, slightly increasing over the years, leaving about 45% of the alumni-formed firms being located in the other 46 states.

MIT alumni firms in the high-growth, high-tech industries (software, electronics, biotech) are particularly likely to locate in California or Massachusetts, especially in the premier technology regions of Silicon Valley and Greater Boston. These two states account for 66% of all MIT alumni electronics firms, 62% of software firms, and 62% of drug and medical firms. By contrast, they are host to only 36% of firms in all other industries.

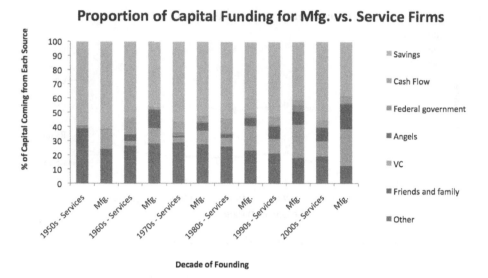

Fig. 2.14 Startup funding, MIT alumni companies (percentage).

2.2.15   Start-up Capital

Most MIT alumni companies are started with funds from the founder's personal savings or by re-investing cash flow, as shown in Figure 2.14. Personal savings was the primary source determined in earlier studies as well (Roberts, 1991, pp. 124–159). Little differences generally exist in the funding patterns across industries or regions of the country, with but a few interesting exceptions. Entrepreneurs' dependence upon personal funds, family and friends, and informal investors (so-called "angels") is not just an MIT-related phenomenon, but seems to have always been true in both the United States and globally.

Strategic corporate partners are important to electronics, machinery, and biotech firms, as well as to chemicals and materials. Meditech, a start-up software firm mentioned above, was an exception to this pattern, in that its initial and primary capital came from EG&G, Inc., a large diversified electronics company, itself a spin-off from MIT formed by an MIT professor and his two graduate assistants, as part of EG&G's efforts to enter the medical technology business.

Venture capital firms are important to software, electronics, and biotech start-ups, as well as to chemicals and materials companies.

In none of these cases, however, were these alternate sources more important at the outset than the founders' own savings. Although venture capital was not a major source of initial or even later funding for smaller firms, it was important as a frequently used source of capital for companies that grew to 50 or more employees, and was even more prominent for those companies that achieved 500 or more workers. This suggests that venture capitalists are good at picking winners, or that venture capital is a necessary tool for a company to become large, or that the venture capitalists provide the companies with critical help, or all three. Although venture capital is now rapidly growing abroad, about 80% of all formal venture capital funding worldwide happens in the United States. Hence, it is not surprising that US MIT alumni start-ups have had higher likelihood of receiving funds from venture capital firms than do the foreign alumni.

2.2.16 Special Case: MIT Alumni Companies in California

We estimate that California has the head offices of 4100 MIT alumni firms, which employ 526,000 people worldwide and have $134 billion in sales. The 2675 MIT alumni firms we project for just northern California account for the greater part of the MIT presence in California — $78 billion in worldwide sales and worldwide employment of 322,100. Total employment of MIT alumni companies in Silicon Valley is estimated at over 260,000 — about half of total California employment of MIT alumni companies. Of this number, 135,200 work in manufacturing companies and 75,500 in the electronics industry.

A 1990 study by the Chase Manhattan Bank identifies 176 MIT alumni-founded companies in northern California (the Silicon Valley area), employing more than 100,000 persons, with aggregate sales then topping $20 billion. The growth over the 16 years since that report until our 2006 data update has been impressive, perhaps attributable, at least in part, to a 1990 underestimation of the number and size of MIT alumni firms. Chase Manhattan noted that a 1924 MIT graduate, Frederick Terman, former dean of engineering at Stanford University, has been acknowledged as the "father of Silicon Valley." Among other achievements accredited to Terman are his role in sponsoring his students, Hewlett and Packard, and the Varian brothers, and his push for the establishment of the Stanford Industrial Park, which helped create a new firms cluster adjacent to Stanford University. Other MIT figures in Silicon Valley's past include: William Shockley 1936, who co-invented the transistor, won the Nobel Prize, and founded Shockley Semiconductor Laboratory, which gave birth to the semiconductor industry; Intel co-founder Robert Noyce 1954, who devised the integrated circuit; William Hewlett, also a 1936 MIT graduate, who co-founded Hewlett-Packard; and Robert Swanson 1969, who co-founded Genentech, the world's first biotechnology company. Owing to their deaths prior to 2003, none of these pioneering individuals or their companies was included in the survey database.

Well over half of the current sales and employment of MIT alumni companies in California is in electronics and instruments, but more than $1 billion in sales are estimated to be in software and biotech. The region's largest MIT alumni firms in the region include Hewlett-Packard, Intel, Synnex, National Semiconductor, 3Com, Qualcomm, Tandem Computer, Raychem, Cirrus Logic, Lam Research, Genentech, Symantec, and VMware.

2.2.17   Case Example: Jacobs and Viterbi — a Pair of California Entrepreneurs[12]

Irwin Jacobs and Andrew Viterbi are both MIT EE, Class of 1957, with Viterbi earning his SB and SM at the same time and Jacobs getting his MIT PhD two years after his master's degree. Jacobs served as an MIT faculty member for several years, whereas Viterbi worked for Raytheon. Both moved to California, Jacobs to become a full professor at the University of California San Diego and Viterbi to work for the Jet Propulsion Lab, also enrolling at the University of Southern California in a PhD program in digital communications. Viterbi too became a faculty member, first at UCLA and later at UCSD, joining Jacobs. Both made major contributions to technology, with Viterbi developing the Viterbi algorithm for data decoding, and both of them

---

[12] Some of the information here comes from http://www.frommittoqualcomm.com/Linkabit/index.html, accessed on March 14, 2011.

later contributing to the development of CDMA wireless and later generations of cell phone chips. In 1968, for the first few months apparently along with another MIT EE alumnus, Leonard Kleinrock 1958, Irwin and Andy co-founded Linkabit Corporation to develop satellite encryption devices, with Jacobs leaving UCSD in 1971 to run the company, and Viterbi departing from UCLA for Linkabit as well. The two of them built Linkabit to $100 million in sales by 1980, with about 1000 employees, heavily dependent upon numerous MIT alumni whom they hired, and then sold it to MA/COM. A total of 75 spin-off companies, direct and indirect, have been traced to the Linkabit alumni!

In 1985, these two close colleagues left MA/COM, along with five others from Linkabit, and co-founded Qualcomm Corporation in San Diego, which has evolved and developed dramatically into a major wireless telecommunications R&D company, gaining significant revenues from patent licensing fees for CDMA and W-CDMA technologies. It is also the largest fabless semiconductor chip supplier in the world. Qualcomm has the somewhat distinct "honor" that China has financed the development of the TDS-CDMA 3G technology precisely to avoid Qualcomm's licensing fees.

In 2010, Qualcomm had revenues of $10.99 billion with 16,500 employees worldwide.

2.2.18 Special Case: MIT in Massachusetts

An estimated 6900 MIT-alumni companies are headquartered in Massachusetts. The estimated sales of these companies — $164 billion — represent 26% of the sales of all Massachusetts companies. Worldwide employment of these 6900 companies is nearly one million, with a substantial share of these jobs spread across the United States and around the world. MIT alumni companies in Massachusetts are located primarily throughout its eastern region.

However, these numbers nevertheless understate the impact of MIT alumni companies on Massachusetts. In one industry after another, these companies have represented cutting-edge technologies in their fields. Historical examples include Raytheon in missile and guidance systems; ThermoElectron (now ThermoFisher Scientific) in instruments and environmental technology; Lotus Development (now part of IBM, so not included in our impact estimates), Medical Information Technology, and Progress Software, all in software; Analog Devices and Analogics in integrated circuits and electronics devices; A123 Systems and American Superconductor in advanced materials; Teradyne in testing equipment for electronic components; BBN and Akamai in telecommunications and networking; Genzyme, Biogen, Alpha-Beta, and Alnylam Pharmaceuticals in biotechnology; Bose in acoustic systems; and AVID in video conferencing. Together, these leading companies have provided a substantial part of the Massachusetts high-tech environment, helping to attract highly skilled professionals and other firms to the state.

One reason MIT is so important to the Massachusetts economy is that, without MIT, most of these companies never would have been located in Massachusetts. Most of the MIT alumni companies in Massachusetts were founded by former students who came to the state to attend MIT, liked what they saw, settled down, and eventually started their companies in Massachusetts. Less than 10% of MIT undergraduates grew up in the state, but approximately 31% of all MIT alumni companies are located in Massachusetts. In the past 5 years, more than 37% of the newly founded MIT alumni companies in software, the Internet, biotech, and electronics have located in Massachusetts.

MIT attracts some of the brightest young people in the country (and the world); many of them enjoy the Boston area and choose to stay there. As just one example, the late Alexander d'Arbeloff (MIT, 1949) came to MIT from Paris just after World War II. His first job after graduation was in New York; however, he chose to come back to Boston, where 11 years later Alex and his MIT undergraduate classmate Nick DeWolf, also Class of 1949, started an electronic testing equipment company in DeWolf's home. When they outgrew the house, they rented space in downtown Boston because they liked living on Beacon Hill and wanted to walk to work. Today, Teradyne has more than a billion dollars in revenues and still is located in the Boston area. Another MIT founder located his company north of Boston; hence, he could have easy access both to downtown and, on weekends, to the Maine coast as well as the New Hampshire mountains. These stories underscore the critical importance of the fact that technically-oriented entrepreneurs like living in the Boston area. Absent the symphony, the parks, the ocean, MIT and other universities, the art museums, and the other cultural and sports attractions that make Boston unique, the city would likely fail to hold these entrepreneurs and the regional economy would grow more slowly or shrink.

Another advantage of locating in Massachusetts is the proximity to MIT and other Boston–Cambridge area universities. When asked the importance of various location factors, Massachusetts firms ranked access to MIT and other universities ahead of low business cost; in every other region of the country, MIT alumni entrepreneurs cited business cost as more important than contact with universities. (As indicated earlier, the most important location factors are quality of life and access to skilled professionals. These factors have average scores well above those for business cost and university access.)

Approximately 32% of the MIT alumni entrepreneurs report having or anticipate having an ongoing connection with MIT. Most frequently, this ongoing connection has taken the form of recruiting new employees, doing joint research, and/or having faculty advisors or directors. The companies of those who graduated more than 30 years ago are slightly less likely to maintain regular contacts than are the most recent graduates.

2.2.19   Case Example: Stata and Lorber — A Pair of Massachusetts Entrepreneurs

Ray Stata 1957 and Matthew Lorber 1956, who shared a Cambridge apartment, started Solid State Instruments in 1961, along with William Linko 1958, with whom they had worked at the MIT Instrumentation Lab. They started the company in the basement of their apartment building, building test devices for gyroscopes, a clear transfer from lessons learned at the I-Lab, whose focus was guidance systems. However, the company did poorly and was sold to Kollmorgen Corporation for $150,000 in stock for the three co-founders and a two-year employment requirement.

While working at Kollmorgen, Ray and Matt began planning their next company, and used their Kollmorgen stock as collateral for a bank loan to finance their start-up, Analog Devices, in 1965. Analog's initial thrust was operational amplifiers, selling into a niche market with little competition. Matt was the initial CEO. By 1969, with sales now passing $6 million, Analog went public, with Lorber selling half his stock and leaving to go on to other ventures. In a recent interview, Ray explained his transition to CEO: "The first thing I did was to stand up in front of all the employees and say, 'I don't have a clue about how to be a president, but I'm going to take the next 12 months to learn. And, if at the end of that 12 months you guys collectively decide, or if the board decides, that I'm not the person who can provide leadership, I'll step down. But in the meantime, while I'm learning, you've got to help me.' So everybody dug in, and there was then no way I could fail. Over the next 12 months I learned how to be a president, and that process has continued for four decades."[13]

That year provided the keys to Analog's future, with purchase of a company that provided entry into analog-to-digital converters, as well as its strategic venture investment in start-up Nova Devices. Two years later, Analog bought Nova, which became its semiconductor division, spurring much of Analog's future growth, with Ray leading the charge during most of that period.

In 2010, Analog Devices, with Stata now as chairman, did $2.8 billion in revenues, with 8500 employees worldwide. Ray had also founded Stata Venture Partners and was aggressively investing in high-tech start-ups in the United States, Israel, India, and China.

---

[13] http://www.ethicsandentrepreneurship.org/20100208/interview-with-ray-stata/, accessed on March 14, 2011.

3

MIT — Its Unique History, Culture, and Entrepreneurial Ecosystem

Global pursuit of research- and technology-based industrial development has mushroomed in the past several decades. Greater Boston's
Route 128 and California's Silicon Valley are the prototypes for other
regions' and other nations' visions of their own futures. But what
caused the original American Technopolis around Greater Boston to
develop? What forces continue today to encourage young local scientists
and engineers to follow entrepreneurial paths. This section of our report
traces the evolution of MIT's and Boston's high-technology community,
indicating the central role of MIT in building entrepreneurial practice
and the supportive entrepreneurial environment or ecosystem. Our own
takeoff from Webster defines an ecosystem as a complex community of
living and non-living things that are functioning together as a unit. We
demonstrate here that such a system has been evolving for at least the
150 years since MIT's founding in 1861 to make entrepreneurship so
vibrant in and around MIT.

Overwhelming anecdotal data argue that the general environment of
the Greater Boston area beginning during the post-World War II period
and, in particular, the atmosphere at MIT have played strong roles
in affecting "would-be" local entrepreneurs. The legitimacy of "useful
work" from MIT's founding days was amplified and directed toward

entrepreneurial expression by prominent early actions taken by administrative and academic leaders. Policies and examples that encouraged faculty and staff involvement with industry and, more important, their "moonlighting" participation in spinning off their ideas and developments into new companies were critical early foundation stones. MIT's tacit approval of entrepreneurism, to some extent even making it the norm, was in our judgment a dramatic, perhaps the defining, contribution to the Greater Boston entrepreneurial culture. Key individual and institutional stimulants such as Stark Draper (MIT, 1926) and the MIT Enterprise Forum reinforced the potential entrepreneurial spin-offs that derived from a wide variety of advanced technology development projects in MIT labs as well as those of other local universities and medical centers, and in the region's high-tech industrial firms. These actions fed into a gradually developing positive feedback loop of productive interactions with the investment community that, in time, created vigorous entrepreneurial activity especially at MIT, and a vital Route 128 community and beyond.

3.1   Early Influences: The Heritage of World War II Science and Technology

The atomic bomb, inertial guided missiles and submarines, computer-based defense of North America, the race to the moon, and the complex of high-technology companies lining the Route 128 highway outside of Boston are phenomena that became prominent in the post-World War II years. This was a time marked by a plethora of scientific and technological advances. The war had identified technology as the critical element upon which the survival of the nation rested, and brought scientists from the shelter of their labs into the confidence of those in the highest levels of government. And in the postwar years, their power and their products and by-products began to shape society, the economy, and the industrial landscape.

How had this started? The sudden need for war research in the early-1940s transformed universities such as MIT into elite research and development centers where the best scientific and technological talent was mobilized for the development of specific practical devices for winning the war. Virtually whole universities redirected their efforts from pure scientific inquiry to the solving of critical problems. While many scientists had to neglect their previous research in favor of war-related innovations, the scientists themselves were not neglected. Science and its offspring technology had become the property of the whole nation with an immediate relevance for all the people.

In addition to the urgent expansion and redirection of university research, the war made necessary the reorganization of research groups, the formation of new working coalitions among scientists and engineers, between these technologists and government officials, and between the universities and industry. These changes were especially noteworthy at MIT, which during the war had become the home of major technological efforts. For example, the MIT Radiation Laboratory, source of many of the major developments in wartime radar, evolved into the postwar MIT Research Laboratory for Electronics. The MIT Servomechanisms Lab, which contributed many advances in automatic control systems, started the research and development project near the end of the war that led to the Whirlwind Computer, created numerically controlled milling machines, and provided the intellectual base for undertaking the MIT Lincoln Laboratory in 1951. After the war, the Servo Lab became the Electronic Systems Lab and continues today as the MIT Laboratory for Information and Decision Systems. Lincoln Lab focused initially on creating a computer-based air defense system (SAGE) to cope with the perceived Soviet threat. To avoid continuing involvement in production and operations once the SAGE system was ready for implementation, MIT spun off a major group from Lincoln Lab to form the non-profit MITRE Corporation, chartered to aid in the later stages of SAGE and to undertake systems analysis for the government. Lincoln then reaffirmed its R&D thrust on computers, communications, radar, and related technologies primarily for the US Department of Defense. The MIT Instrumentation Lab, growing out of the wartime gun-sight work of Professor Charles Stark Draper, its founder and director throughout his career at MIT, continued its efforts on the R&D needed to create inertial guidance systems for aircraft, submarines, and missiles. It followed up with significant achievements in the race to the moon with developments of the guidance and stellar navigation systems for the

Apollo program. The former Instrumentation Lab now bears Draper's name in its spunoff-from-MIT non-profit status. Draper testified as to the scope of these endeavors: "Personal satisfaction... was greatest when projects included all essential phases, ranging from imaginative conception, through theoretical analysis and engineering to documentation for manufacture, supervision of small-lot production, and, finally, monitoring of applications to operational situations." All these MIT labs were spawned during a period in which little debate existed about a university's appropriate response to national urgency. They have successfully fulfilled their defined missions, while also providing a base of advanced technology programs and people for other possible societal roles, importantly including significant entrepreneurial birthing.

3.2   Building on a Tradition

The World War II efforts and the immediate postwar involvements of MIT with major national problems built upon a much older tradition at MIT, enunciated by its founder William Barton Rogers in 1861 when he created an institution to "respect the dignity of useful work." MIT's slogan is "Mens et Manus," Latin for "mind and hand," and its traditional logo shows the scholar and the craftsman in parallel positions. For a long time, MIT was seen as virtually alone as a university that embraced rather than shunned industry. Early alumni of "Boston Tech" (what MIT was "fondly" called before its move from Boston to Cambridge in 1910) pioneered new industries, such as automobiles. For example, Aurin Chase, MIT class of 1900, soon after in 1906 founded and ran Chase Motor Truck Company, a major truck and track vehicle supplier to the US Army during World War I. From its start, MIT had developed close ties with technology-based industrialists, such as Thomas Edison and Alexander Graham Bell, then later with its illustrious alumnus Alfred P. Sloan (MIT, 1892) during his pioneering years at General Motors, and with close ties to the growing US petroleum industry. In 1930s, MIT generated The Technology Plan to link industry with MIT in what became the first and is still the largest university–industry collaborative, the MIT Industrial Liaison Program. In 2010, it had close to 200 of the world's leading research- and technology-based companies as its members.

The wartime leadership of MIT's distinguished president, Karl Taylor Compton, accelerated these precedents by bringing MIT into intimacy with the war effort while he headed all national R&D coordination in Washington. Then, in the immediate postwar years, Compton pioneered efforts toward commercial use of military developments, among other things helping to create the first institutionalized venture capital fund, American Research and Development (AR&D).

"AR&D was, in part, the brainchild of Compton, then head of MIT. In discussions with Merrill Griswold, Chairman of Massachusetts Investors Trust [a quite different MIT], and Senator Ralph Flanders of Vermont, then President of the Federal Reserve Bank of Boston, Compton pointed out that some of the A-bomb technology that had been bottled up for four years had important industrial applications. At the same time, it was apparent to Griswold and Flanders that much of New England's wealth was in the hands of insurance companies and trusts with no outlet to creative enterprises. Griswold and Flanders organized AR&D in June 1946 to supply new enterprise capital to New England entrepreneurs. (Compton became a board member, MIT became an initial investor, and a scientific advisory board was established that included three MIT department heads.) General Georges Doriot, who was professor of industrial management at Harvard, was later asked to become president" (Ziegler, 1982, p. 152). AR&D's first several investments were in MIT developments, and some of the emerging companies were housed initially in MIT facilities. For example, in 1947 AR&D invested in High Voltage Engineering Corporation, which was located in the so-called "back lot" of MIT to take advantage of Professor John Trump's (MIT, 1933) Van de Graaf generator that stood there. AR&D also invested in Ionics Inc., which became the United States' pre-eminent water purification company, purchased by General Electric in 2004 for $1.3 billion, but housed initially in the basement of the MIT Chemical Engineering building. MIT provided the space, heat, and light, and AR&D paid for the staff and out-of-pocket R&D expenses. That kind of arrangement was certainly most unusual for its time, albeit quite entrepreneurial, and today would be seen at most universities, including MIT, as a source of controversy and potential conflict. Compton's successor as president of MIT, James Killian (MIT, 1926), furthered the encouragement of entrepreneurial efforts by MIT faculty and staff as well as close ties with both industry and government. At various times Killian served on the boards of both General Motors and IBM and as President Eisenhower's Science Advisor.

The traditions of MIT involvement with industry long since had been legitimatized in its official "Rules and Regulations of the Faculty," encouraging active consulting by faculty members of about one day per week and, more impressive for its time, approving faculty part-time efforts in forming and building their own companies, a practice still questioned at many universities. Early faculty-founded companies include Arthur D. Little, Inc. (ADL), Edgerton Germeshausen and Grier (EG&G, Inc.), Bolt Beranek & Newman (BBN, Inc.), and many others. Initially, these were consulting firms that only later extended their domains into the realm of products. Faculty entrepreneurship, carried out over the years with continuing and occasionally heightened reservations about potential conflicts of interest, generally was extended to the research staff as well, who were thereby enabled to "moonlight" while being "full-time" employees of MIT labs and departments. The result is that a large fraction of all MIT spin-off enterprises, including essentially all faculty-initiated companies and many staff-founded firms, are started on a part-time basis, smoothing the way for many entrepreneurs to "test the waters" of high-tech entrepreneurship before making a full plunge. These companies are obvious candidates for most direct movement of laboratory technology into the broader markets not otherwise served by MIT.

Few of the faculty founders, including Amar Bose 1951, founder of Bose Corporation, or Robert Langer 1974, a brilliant biomaterials scientist who has co-founded more than 20 companies, or Phil Sharp, Nobel prize winner and co-founder of Biogen in 1978 and Alnylam Pharmaceuticals in 2002, ever resigned their MIT positions. They preferred to remain at MIT for years, carrying on their research and teaching, while turning over the full-time reins to their former graduate students and lab colleagues. That pattern is so familiar at MIT that a quarterly meeting hosted for entrepreneurial alumni by former MIT President Paul Gray 1954, and called "The Technology Breakfast," has long had the format of starting with an MIT faculty member who discusses his or her research work that was later commercialized, then followed by usually a former graduate student who led the early stages of new company creation based upon the technology. George Hatsopoulos 1949, founder of ThermoElectron Corporation, Jay Barger 1950, co-founder with another faculty colleague of Dynatech, Alan Michaels 1944, founder of Amicon, and Tom Gerrity 1963, co-founder of Index Systems, are among the few faculty who left to pursue their entrepreneurial endeavors on a full-time basis, with great success achieved in all four cases.

Although today regional and national governments on a worldwide basis seek to emulate the Boston-area pattern of technological entrepreneurship, in the early years the MIT traditions spread to other institutions very slowly. The principal early disciple was Frederick Terman 1924, who took his Cambridge experiences as an MIT PhD student back to Stanford University, forsaking a faculty offer by MIT, to lead Stanford eventually into technological excellence. From his earlier MIT studies, amplified by his WWII service in Cambridge, Terman gained first-hand exposure to the close ties between MIT and industry, made more important to him by his being mentored by Professor Vannevar Bush 1916, later dean of engineering and then vice president of MIT, who participated in founding American Appliance Company, later renamed Raytheon Corporation, to work on radio components. The attitudes Terman developed while at MIT led him to encourage and guide his former students, such as William Hewlett (MIT, 1936) and David Packard and the Varian brothers, to start their high-technology firms and eventually to locate them next to the university in the newly formed Stanford Research Park. While these efforts obviously helped found what has become known as "Silicon Valley," the resulting early proliferation of firms there came heavily from multiple spin-offs of other companies, and did not follow the dominant Greater Boston pattern of direct fostering of new firms from MIT labs and departments. The MIT-Route 128 model still today remains unusual in its degree of regional entrepreneurial dependence upon one major academic institution.

3.3 The Neighboring Infrastructure

Yet, MIT has not been alone over the past several decades in nurturing the technology-based community of Boston, an entrepreneurial ecosystem now sprawling outward beyond Route 128 to the newer Route 495. Northeastern University, a large urban institution with heavy engineering enrollment and an active co-operative education program with industry, has educated many aspiring engineers who provided both support staff and entrepreneurs to the growing area. Every year the MIT Instrumentation Laboratory employed many Northeastern engineering co-op students, not accidentally exposing them to the entrepreneurial culture of the I-Lab. Richard Egan worked there for a number of years, on co-op and then full-time, helping to develop memory systems for Apollo guidance as part of the NASA moon program. Dick received the bachelor's degree from Northeastern and later in 1963 his master's degree in electrical engineering from MIT. Years later Egan (the "E") co-founded EMC Corporation with his Northeastern undergraduate roommate, Roger Marino (the "M"), not surprisingly focused upon memory systems!

Similarly, another local Boston technical university, Wentworth Institute, educates many of the technicians needed to support the development efforts at both the MIT university labs and the spin-off companies. Boston University and Tufts University, both with strong science and engineering faculties, also play important roles. Even small liberal arts Brandeis University has participated, with Professor Orrie Friedman in 1961 starting Collaborative Research, Inc., forerunner of the much later biotechnology boom in the Greater Boston area. And that firm also illustrates the beginnings of cross-institutional ties among faculty entrepreneurs, with MIT Professor David Baltimore becoming the Chief Scientist of Collaborative while in his young 30s. Baltimore later became the founding director of the MIT Whitehead Institute, a major building block of the Cambridge biotech entrepreneurial cluster, and still later President of the Rockefeller University, then President of the California Institute of Technology, a Nobel Prize winner, and a co-founder of several companies.

Possibly surprising to readers from outside of the Boston area, Harvard University did not have a substantial role in entrepreneurial endeavors until the recent biotechnology revolution, in which Harvard Medical School and its affiliated teaching hospitals are playing a major role. In many ways Harvard, over the years, has looked down its "classics" nose with disdain at the "crass commercialism" of its technological neighbor a few miles down the Charles River. An Wang, who had worked at the Harvard Computation Laboratory before founding Wang Laboratories, Inc., is the most prominent exception to this rule.

However, change in regard to encouraging entrepreneurship has been in the wind over the past two decades, even at Harvard. The outpouring of excellent research and discovery from Harvard's Chemistry and Biology Departments, as well as from the Harvard Medical School across the river in Boston, has caused Harvard faculty and staff recently to become much more active and successful participants in entrepreneurial start-ups, although not without voiced reluctance and controversy at the university. In fact, in a dramatic early attempted revolution of its policies, Harvard asked Professor of Biochemistry Mark Ptashne to start Genetics Institute in 1979, a company in which Harvard would hold 15–20% equity (something MIT has never done!). However, protest by critics as to possible influence of such ownership caused Harvard to pull out. Ptashne went ahead and formed the company, while still remaining on the Harvard University faculty. In 1989, the Harvard Medical School took the far reaching step of organizing a venture capital fund (discontinued a few years later) to invest in new companies whose founders related to Harvard Medical, in some ways mimicking MIT's much earlier but less direct activities in regard to AR&D, but nevertheless a pioneering step among academic institutions. And recently a group of Harvard Medical-affiliated hospitals (Partners Healthcare) has formed its own venture capital firm that is investing actively in its commercial spin-off companies, especially from the MGH and the Brigham & Women's Hospital, both renowned medical research and patient care institutions.

Some key MIT "cross-overs" to Harvard are helping to change the environment and the outcomes there. George Whitesides, one of America's most distinguished chemists, began his academic career at MIT, served as a faculty member and Department Chair from 1963 to 1982, co-founded his first companies while at MIT, and then moved his lab and his energies to Harvard University, where he has continued starting and building companies. The web site of one of his current companies, Nano-Terra,[1] where Whitesides is Chairman, indicates: "Dr. Whitesides is a co-founder of companies with a combined market capitalization of over \$20 billion. In the early 1980s, he co-founded biotechnology company Genzyme, which remains one of the world's leading biotechnology companies [recently sold to Sanofi-Aventis for \$20 billion]; in 1993 he co-founded GelTex, which was acquired by Genzyme for \$1.2 billion; and in 1996, he co-founded Theravance, which went public in 2004 and currently has a \$1.1B market capitalization. Professor Whitesides' more recent ventures include Surface Logix and WMR Biomedical." The growing cross-institutional ties are reflected even in Nano-Terra, where Dr. Carmichael Roberts, an MIT Sloan MBA recipient in 2000, is Vice Chairman. The web site indicates that Carmichael and Whitesides are co-founders of Surface Logix, Arsenal Medical, and Diagnostics For All.

Another entrepreneurial transfer from MIT to Harvard is Kent Bowen (MIT, 1971), who received his PhD and became an MIT Materials Science & Engineering faculty member and entrepreneur for 22 years before he moved to the Harvard Business School. Among other activities since arriving at Harvard is his co-founding with George Whitesides and Carmichael Roberts of Diagnostics for All, listed above, which won the 2008 MIT \$100K Business Plan Competition, as will be discussed later. These people transfers from MIT to other universities also clearly create role models for their faculty colleagues as well as for their students, with impact that will extend over long periods of time. They also contribute to the gradual changes in institutional culture that eventually matter most. As an example, in 2010 a major change took place at Harvard and at the Harvard Business School that is likely to impact the neighborhood's entrepreneurship. HBS appointed a new Dean, Nitin Nohria (MIT, 1988), who received his PhD from MIT Sloan, where he was educated with full visibility of the extensive entrepreneurship at MIT and daily involvement with all of the faculty and programs of the MIT Entrepreneurship Center. In his first few months as Dean, Nohria announced participation in a university-wide Harvard Innovation Laboratory, located at its business

---

[1] http://www.nanoterra.com/leadership.asp, accessed on February 9, 2011.

school. Not surprisingly, Professor George Whitesides was present at the announcement.

In earlier years, encouraged no doubt by the unique venture capitalist role of Professor Doriot, and separated by the Charles River from main campus influence, some Harvard Business School graduates found welcome homes in even the early high-tech company developments. As our MIT survey revealed, the same experiences were occurring for alumni of the long-standing MIT undergraduate management program and, after its 1951 founding, from the MIT Sloan graduate school as well. These business school graduates got involved in start-up teams initially as administrators and sales people, but in more recent years participated frequently as primary founders. Thus, Aaron Kleiner '69, from the MIT Sloan School of Management shares the founding of at least nine high-technology companies with his MIT computer science undergraduate roommate, Raymond Kurzweil '70. Their companies generally reflected the artificial intelligence technologies of pattern recognition, generating products such as the Kurzweil reading machine for the blind and the Kurzweil music synthesizer. And Robert Metcalfe '68 combined MIT educational programs in both engineering and management prior to his invention of the Ethernet and launch of 3Com. The Greater Boston environment has become so tuned to entrepreneurship that even student projects with local companies, a part of routine course work in every local management school, have ended up helping to create numerous entrepreneurial launches. Several firms evolved from feasibility studies done as part of Doriot's famed "Manufacturing" course at the Harvard Business School. And *INC.* magazine founder, Bernard Goldhirsh '61, credited an MIT Sloan School marketing course with confirming for him the huge market potential for a magazine targeted toward entrepreneurs and small business managers.

Boston entrepreneurs also eventually benefited from understanding bankers and private investors, each group setting examples to be emulated later in other parts of the country. The First National Bank of Boston (later becoming BankBoston and now part of Bank of America) had begun in the 1950s to lend money to early stage firms based on receivables from government R&D contracts, a move seen at the time as extremely risky even though the loans seemed to be entirely secured.

Arthur Snyder, then vice president of commercial lending of the New England Merchants Bank (which became Bank of New England and later part of Citizens Bank), regularly took out full page ads in the *Boston Globe* that showed himself with an aircraft or missile model in his hands, calling upon high-technology entrepreneurs to see him about their financial needs. Snyder even set up a venture capital unit at the bank (one of the first in the United States) to make small equity investments in high-tech companies to which he had loaned money.

Several scions of old Boston Brahmin families became personally involved in venture investments even in the earliest time periods. For example, in 1946, William Coolidge helped arrange the financing for Tracerlab, MIT's first nuclear-oriented spin-off company, eventually introducing William Barbour (MIT, 1933) of Tracerlab to AR&D, which carried out the needed investment (Ziegler, 1982, p. 151). Coolidge also invested in National Research Corporation (NRC), a company founded by MIT alumnus Richard Morse '33 (later the first teacher of entrepreneurship at MIT) to exploit advances in low-temperature physics. The leaders of NRC later created several companies from its labs, retaining partial ownership in each as they spun off, the most important being Minute Maid orange juice, later sold to Coca Cola. NRC's former headquarters building, constructed adjacent to MIT on Memorial Drive in Cambridge, now houses the primary classrooms of the MIT Sloan School of Management. Incidentally, long before the construction of Route 128, Memorial Drive used to be called "Multi-Million Dollar Research Row" because of the several early high-technology firms next to MIT, including NRC, Arthur D. Little Inc., and Electronics Corporation of America (ECA). ECA's old site at One Memorial Drive, adjacent to MIT Sloan, now houses Microsoft's regional development center, as well as numerous start-ups and venture capital firms.

The comfortable and growing ties between Boston's worlds of academia and finance helped create bridges to the large Eastern family fortunes — the Rockefellers, Whitneys, and Mellons, among others — who also invested in early Boston start-ups. Although these funds existed, they were not available in generous amounts. Even in 1958, Ken Olsen (MIT, 1950) (who died recently) and Harlan Anderson '53 had to surrender more than 70% of start-up DEC for the $70,000 they received from AR&D.

Other aspects of the surrounding infrastructure were also slow in happening. By and large, lawyers were uninformed about high-tech deals, and general law firms had no specialists in intellectual property. As late as the early-1980s, the MIT and Harvard co-founders of Zero Stage Capital, Boston's first "seed capital" fund, eventually found Paul Brontas, the senior partner of Boston's then leading law firm Hale & Dorr (now part of the national WilmerHale firm), to be among the only lawyers in town who knew how to set up the complex structure of a venture capital firm. One of the few other well-known lawyers in the early Boston high-tech community was Richard Testa, senior partner of Testa, Hurwitz & Thibeault. Dick was very close to American Research & Development, and Testa became the legal (and more) underpinning of numerous of the firms in which AR&D invested and many others. His law firm eventually built the most prominent Boston-based practice in the high-tech area, and thrived until shortly after Dick's early death in 2002.

By the end of the 1940s, when space constraints in the inner cities of Boston and Cambridge might have begun to be burdensome for continuing growth of an emerging high-technology industrial base, the state highway department launched the building of Route 128, a circumferential highway (Europeans and Asians would call it a "ring road") around Boston, through pig farms and small communities. Route 128 made suburban living more readily accessible and land available in large quantities and at low prices. MIT Lincoln Lab's establishment in 1951 in Concord, previously known only as the site of the initial 1776 Lexington–Concord Revolutionary War battle with the British, "the shot heard round the world," or, to some, as the home of Thoreau's Walden Pond, helped bring advanced technology to the suburbs. Today Route 128, proudly labeled by Massachusetts as "America's Technology Highway," reflects the cumulative evidence of more than 60 years of industrial growth of electronics, computer, and software companies. Development planners in some foreign countries have occasionally been confused by consultants and/or state officials into believing that the once convenient, now traffic-clogged, Route 128 highway system actually caused the technological growth of the Greater Boston area. At best the Route 128 highway itself, later followed by the more distant Route 495 circumferential road, has been a moderate facilitator of the development of this high-technology region. More likely the so-called "Route 128 phenomenon" is a result and a beneficiary of the growth caused by the other influences identified earlier.

3.4   Accelerating Upward from the Base: Positive Feedback

A critical influence on entrepreneurship in Greater Boston (and we assert in other regions as well, when they do indeed take off) is the effect of "positive feedback" arising from the early role models and successes. (Today's social and economics jargon for the engineer's "positive feedback loop" is a "virtuous cycle," when the overall effects seem to be beneficial, and a "vicious cycle," when the impact is harmful!) Entrepreneurship, especially when successful, begets more entrepreneurship. Schumpeter (1936, p. 198) observed: "The greater the number of people who have already successfully founded new businesses, the less difficult it becomes to act as an entrepreneur. It is a matter of experience that successes in this sphere, as in all others, draw an ever-increasing number of people in their wake." This has certainly been true at MIT. The earliest faculty founders were senior faculty of high academic repute at the times they started their firms. Their initiatives as entrepreneurs were evidences for others at MIT and nearby that technical entrepreneurship was a legitimate activity to be undertaken by strong technologists and leaders. Karl Compton's unique role in co-founding AR&D while president of MIT furthered this image, as did the MIT faculty's efforts in bringing early-stage developments to AR&D's attention. Obviously, "if they can do it, then so can I" might well have been a rallying cry for junior faculty and staff, as well as for engineers in local large firms. Our comparative study years ago of Swedish and Massachusetts technological entrepreneurs found that on average the US entrepreneurs could name about 10 other new companies before they started their own, three or four of which were in the same general area of high-technology business. Few of the Swedish entrepreneurs could name even one or two others like themselves. A prospective entrepreneur gains

Table 3.1. Role of MIT's positive feedback loop in venture founding (from limited sample only).

Proportion of founders who chose MIT because of its entrepreneurial environment (percentage)				
Graduation decade	1950s $(N=207)$	1960s $(N=313)$	1970s $(N=373)$	1980s $(N=315)$	1990s $(N=214)$
Chose MIT because of its entrepreneurial reputation	17	12	19	26	42

comfort from having visibility of others like herself or himself, this evidence more likely if local entrepreneurship has a critical mass, making the individual's break from conventional employment less threatening.

The positive feedback loop affecting MIT's entrepreneurial output is no doubt most affected by the increasing attraction of the Institute to students, staff, and faculty who are entrepreneurially inclined even before they arrive. The more entrepreneurial that MIT appears to be, the more that potential entrepreneurs want to be there. Table 3.1 indicates the responses from those MIT alumni entrepreneurs who completed the 2003 survey. Clearly, for more than 50 years, MIT has been attractive to those who later form new companies. The table also shows an amazing escalation over the past 30 years. Indeed, 42% of those 1990s graduates who already have formed companies within their very first decade out of MIT claim they were attracted to MIT originally by its reputed entrepreneurial environment. The more entrepreneurs MIT produces, the stronger the entrepreneurial environment and reputation, the more likely entrepreneurs, both students and faculty, are attracted to come to MIT! (No data exist to prove this claimed historic effect upon the MIT faculty, but the authors are willing to bet that it is true!)

The growing early entrepreneurial developments at MIT and, more broadly, in the Greater Boston area also encouraged their brave investors and brought other wealthy individuals forward to participate. As an example of the spiraling growth of new firms, even in the early days, Ziegler (1982) shows the proliferation of 13 nuclear-related companies "fissioning" within 15 years from Tracerlab's 1946 founding, including Industrial Nucleonics (which became Accuray),

Tech Ops, and New England Nuclear (purchased by DuPont). MIT alumni-founded Tracerlab and many of its progeny. Inevitably, that led not only to more new firms but to a technological cluster of companies that interacted with each other to the benefit of all. With now over 50 years of intensive regional entrepreneurial activity in the Boston area, a positive feedback loop of new company formation has generated significant outcomes, even if the initial rate of growth was slow. In the mid-1960s, through dramatic proliferation of spin-off companies, Fairchild Semiconductor (co-founded by MIT alumnus, Robert Noyce '53, before he left to co-found Intel) gave birth to similar and rapid positive feedback that launched the semiconductor industry in Silicon Valley. And Tracor, Inc. provided a comparable impetus to new company formation, especially in military electronics, in Austin, Texas.

A side benefit of this growth, also feeding back to help it along, is the development of supporting infrastructure in the region — technical, legal, accounting, banking, and real estate — all better understanding how to serve the needs of young technological firms. In Nancy Dorfman's early (1983) assessment of the economic impact of the Boston-area developments, she observes "a network of job shoppers that supply made-to-order circuit boards, precision machinery, metal parts and sub-assemblies, as well as electronic components, all particularly critical to new start-ups that are developing prototypes and to manufacturers of customized equipment for small markets. In addition, dozens if not hundreds of consulting firms, specializing in hardware and software, populate the region to serve new firms and old." Of course, this massive network is itself made up of many of the entrepreneurial firms we have been investigating. Within this infrastructure in the Boston area are now "not-so-new" "networking" organizations, such as the MIT Enterprise Forum (to be discussed later) and the 128 Venture Group, which bring together on a monthly or even more frequent basis entrepreneurs, investors, and other participants in the entrepreneurial community, contributing further positive loop gain.

3.5   Technology Clusters

This positive feedback effect certainly occurred in the Greater Boston region as a whole and, as illustrated by the Tracerlab and Fairchild examples, also frequently occurs in many places at the single organizational level. As one individual or group departs a given lab or company to form a new enterprise, the entrepreneurial phenomenon may mushroom and tend to perpetuate itself among others who learn about the spin-off and also get the idea of leaving. Sometimes one group of potential entrepreneurs feels it is better suited than its predecessors to exploit a particular idea or technology, stimulating the second group to follow quickly. Five different groups left the Draper Lab over a two-year period to establish new companies based upon the lab's advances in micro-electronics. The "outside environment" can help this process by becoming more conducive to additional new enterprise formation. In particular, venture capitalists, learning more about a "source organization" of new ideas and/or key people from the organization's earlier spin-offs, may actively seek to encourage further spin-offs from the same source.

3.5.1 The Biotechnology Cluster

This positive feedback process certainly played an important role in the 1980s' beginning of the still-continuing proliferation of biotechnology spin-offs from MIT and Harvard academic departments and medical centers. Sometimes a "keystone" company assists many others to be formed, as was done by BioInformation Associates, a company formed by eight MIT professors, including Anthony Sinskey '67 and Charles Cooney '70, to provide technical and strategic assistance to others interested in starting new biotechnology firms. It helped significantly in the creation and development of Genzyme Corporation, among others, which was sold in the beginning of 2011 to Sanofi-Aventis for $20 billion. And the increasing critical mass of companies and their skilled scientists and engineers attract other companies, even very large global firms such as Novartis, to locate laboratories and other facilities in the midst of the clusters, enhancing the availability of scientists and engineers, and further strengthening the relevant infrastructure.

As evidences of the results that come from this positive feedback effect within a given industry, we show two local maps of the area near MIT. The first, Figure 3.1, indicates the recent status of the biotechnology cluster in and around Kendall Square, Cambridge, within blocks of

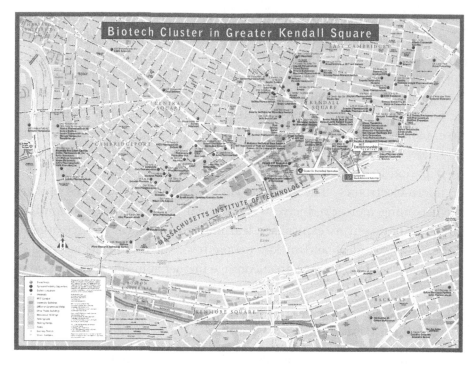

Fig. 3.1 Biotech companies clustered in Greater Kendall Square, Cambridge MA. (*Source*: MIT Entrepreneurship Center study, March 2008).

MIT. A total of 95 biotech companies had been documented by early-2008 as located within this complex, compared with 55 just three years prior. Thirteen of the Kendall Square life sciences companies accounted for two-thirds of the $1.8 billion Massachusetts companies spent on R&D in 2000. By the year 2001, 21 of the Kendall Square companies either were founded by MIT alumni or faculty, or had MIT-licensed technology; their revenues were $2.5 billion.

Since 2001, the biotech numbers have continued to grow substantially. In ongoing research on the MIT-related life sciences complex in Cambridge, Professor Fiona Murray of MIT Sloan found that 66 of the 493 MIT "life scientists" (including those at the affiliated Broad and Whitehead Institutes) have founded or served on the Board of Directors of at least one venture-funded company, totaling 134 companies in all. Eighteen of these faculty or staff have founded or been Board members of at least three companies each, with one MIT faculty member having 20 such relationships. Fifty additional MIT "life science" people serve as a science advisory board member of an additional 108 companies, bringing a total of at least 242 life-science companies into strong ties with the MIT community. These ties are both cause and result of the interconnections between MIT and the entrepreneurial and industrial community. A large fraction of these life sciences faculty, post docs, and staff do not have MIT degrees and therefore are not counted among the MIT alumni entrepreneurship firms discussed in the earlier part of this report. Therefore, the economic and technological impact of these companies, by and large, supplement the data presented in the beginning of this report.

Another sign of linkage of this cluster to MIT is the record of biotech/biomedical winners and runners up in the MIT $100K Competition (and its predecessors, the $10K and the $50K), the annual student-run business plan competition that will be discussed later in greater depth. Data compiled by the MIT Entrepreneurship Center, listed in Table 3.2, show 18 bio-related companies in the past 14 years,

Table 3.2.   Recent biotech/biomed MIT $50K–$100K leaders.

Company	Year	Outcome
Privo Technologies	2010	Finalist
Diagnostics for All	2008	Winner
Robopsy	2007	Winner
Sempus BioSciences (SteriCoat)	2006	Winner
Invivo Therapeutics	2005	Finalist
Balico	2005	Winner
Myomo (Active Joint Brace)	2004	Winner
SmartCells	2003	Winner
Ancora Pharmaceuticals	2002	Finalist
Crosslink Medical	2002	Finalist
Angstrom Medical	2001	Winner
Iptyx	2001	Finalist
SiteSpecific Pharma	2001	Finalist
SmartCure	2001	Finalist
EyeGen	2000	Winner
MolecularWare	1999	Winner
Virtmed	1998	Finalist
Actuality Systems	1997	Winner

several of which became real companies following their MIT $100K successes.

3.5.2   Case Example: SmartCells

Todd Zion '04, approaching the end of his PhD program in Chemical Engineering, saw the MIT $50K competition as a possible source of prize money to help start a company, as well as providing increased visibility to potential investors. He quickly assembled a team consisting of his good friend and PhD classmate, Tom Lancaster '04, plus two students from MIT Sloan and two more from the Harvard Business School. The business idea was Todd's doctoral dissertation topic, a unique way to deliver to a diabetic patient a "smart insulin" that responds to the patient's own blood glucose level, releasing the insulin when a patient needs it. And they won the 2003 $30,000 Robert Goldberg Grand Prize.

Todd (CEO) and Tom (Director of Chemistry, and later VP R&D) founded SmartCells, Inc., joined by Jim Harriman (VP Operations, and later CFO), who had been recommended by their advisors from the MIT Venture Mentoring Service (Section 5.1). The $30,000 in prize money was spent largely in legal fees to get started, including licensing Todd's dissertation technology from the MIT TLO (Section 4.3).

SmartCells took the rather unusual path at that time, especially for a bio-related start-up, of avoiding venture capital investors, focusing entirely on angel investors and government grants. In fact, Todd applied for his first National Institutes of Health (NIH) grant even before he completed his PhD, and received the funding shortly after incorporation. For Todd's first equity round, he fortunately found several individual champions, such as Jonathan Fleming, MIT Senior Lecturer in Entrepreneurship and CEO of Oxford Bioscience Ventures, as well as key players in two local angel groups, Boston Harbor Angels and Angel Healthcare. The company was off and running.

SmartCells stuck to this funding strategy while moving forward with its R&D program. Over its seven years, it raised nearly $10 million from angels and close to $12 million in grants, including in 2008 some funds from the Juvenile Diabetes Research Foundation. This strategy preserved the bulk of ownership of the company for its founders and other employees.

In 2008, the company began to explore the interests of major pharmaceutical companies in possible alliances or acquisitions. Those talks became serious in 2010, when SmartCells was preparing to run its "first-in-man" studies. Negotiations with several major firms generated four term sheets.

In December 2010, Merck announced that it was acquiring Smart-Cells, Inc. for a substantial upfront cash payment and contingent milestone payments that could total over $500 million. No mention was made in Merck's press release of the royalty payments that might accrue if the SmartInsulin products reach the market.

3.5.3   The Energy Cluster

A second cluster has formed rapidly in the energy field. Over the past five decades, 3% of MIT entrepreneurs classified their firms as in the energy sector. We now estimate that MIT alumni are creating 30–35 new energy-focused firms every year. Several hundred companies are in the New England energy cluster, with 263 in Massachusetts alone by early-2008. In Figure 3.2, we show the Boston Metropolitan portion, containing 22 energy companies in Cambridge and 25 more in Boston. The broad geographic distribution of the energy firms, relative to the

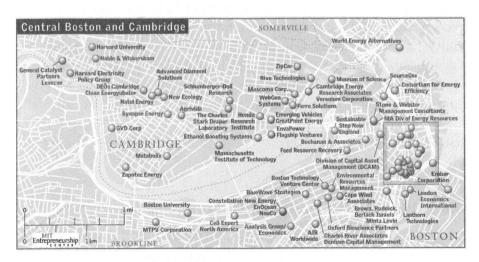

Fig. 3.2 The emerging energy cluster in Greater Boston.
(*Source*: MIT Entrepreneurship Center study, April 2008).

biotech companies shown in Figure 3.1, reflects the large number of source organizations of the energy companies, their wide diversity of technological bases, and their need for somewhat greater physical space than is readily available in central Cambridge. A high percentage of the new energy firms are MIT-related in terms of their founders and/or technology sources.

As also discussed in our later section on MIT entrepreneurship clubs, our now current Managing Director of the MIT Entrepreneurship Center, William Aulet '94, working as part of the MIT Energy Initiative in 2006, began to develop a comprehensive program to address the challenge of Clean Energy Entrepreneurship. This included new MIT curricular offerings, encouragement of student clubs, periodic MIT events, and the $200K MIT Clean Energy Prize, sponsored by the US Department of Energy and NSTAR, the major New England regional utility. This series of coordinated efforts has resulted in a dramatic and continuing increase in the number and quality of newly formed energy-related companies. What had started as an extension into the clean energy domain of the MIT $100K Business Plan Competition "went national" soon thereafter, gaining entrants from universities all across the United States. For 2011, 81 entering teams from 47 US universities are participating in this competition. As a result of all of this activity, in 2009, the Global Consortium of Entrepreneurship Centers recognized the MIT Entrepreneurship Center for its Excellence in Specialty Entrepreneurship Education in Energy. In 2010, the Cleantech Group named MIT the top "cleantech" innovation and entrepreneurship university in the United States and cited it as a "true clean tech spin-off machine." That designation went global when, in 2011, the CleanTechies web site rated the MIT Clean Energy Prize #1 in its list of the "Top Ten University Clean Energy Initiatives Around the Globe."

3.6   Other "Pulls" on Potential Entrepreneurs

In addition to the general environmental encouragements on technological entrepreneurship in MIT's surroundings, specific "pulls" are at work on some of the people, making entrepreneurship an attractive goal to attain. Such influences may inhere in the general atmosphere of a particular organization, making it more conducive to the new enterprise spin-off process. For example, until his recent death, Stark Draper '26, visionary leader of the MIT Instrumentation Laboratory (later renamed the Draper Lab), was a key source of encouragement to anyone who came in contact with him. No wonder that the National Academy of Engineering established the Draper Prize to be the equivalent in engineering of the Nobel Prizes in science. Having had the good fortune to fly coast-to-coast with Draper one night on a "red eye" from Los Angeles, one of our co-authors learned much about Draper's unique attitudes toward developing young technologists.

> "I try to assign project managers who are just a bit shy of being ready for the job," Draper said. "That keeps them really hopping when the work gets underway, although the government officials usually want to wring my neck."
>
> "I break up successful teams once they've received their honors. That way every one remembers them for their success, rather than for some later failure. Also, this causes every young person in the Lab to be sitting within one hundred feet of someone who's had his hand shaken by the President of the United States."
>
> "The Lab is a place for young people to learn. Then they can go someplace else to succeed."

"When I give speeches I single out those who have already left the Lab — to become professors elsewhere, VPs of Engineering in industry, or founders of their own companies. Staying behind in the lab is just for a few old 'beezers' like me who have no place else to go!" Draper's organizational environment was one of high achievement, but with negative incentives for remaining too long. Salaries flattened out quickly, causing the income gap between staying and leaving to grow rapidly as an engineer gained experience. Engineers completing a project had a sharp breakpoint, a good time for someone confident from the success of his or her project to spin off. In retrospect, Stark Draper clearly consciously tried to encourage spin-offs of all sorts from his laboratory, perhaps the highest attainment achievable by an academic scientist.

No questions were asked if Instrumentation Lab employees wanted to borrow equipment to take home over the weekend, and many of them began their new companies "moonlighting" with this kind of undisguised blessing. Draper wanted reasonably high levels of turnover, and constant introduction to the Lab of bright, eager, young people. Over a 15-year period during which we traced Lab performance, the average age of Instrumentation Laboratory employees remained at 33 years, plus or minus six months. This young-age stability, maintaining the lab's vitality and fighting off technological obsolescence, was not true at most of the other MIT labs we studied.

Draper apparently produced similar effects in his teaching activities at MIT. Tom Gerrity '63, founder of Index Systems, which, in turn, later created Index Technology and Applied Expert Systems as sponsored spinouts, reports that Draper's undergraduate elective subject showed him the importance of being able to put together lots of different skills and disciplines to produce a result. Gerrity adopted this systems point of view in co-founding Index several years later, after three MIT degrees and a stint as a faculty member in the MIT Sloan School of Management. Still later, Gerrity became Dean of the Wharton School of the University of Pennsylvania.

Some other MIT laboratory directors followed similar patterns of entrepreneurial "sponsorship" in smaller, less-well-known labs. For example, the head of the Aero-elastic and Structures Laboratory of the MIT Department of Aeronautics and Astronautics had the attitude that the lab provided an internship type of position and that staff members were more or less expected to move on after a reasonable period. In other labs, the environment just seemed to breed entrepreneurism. Douglas Ross '54, who left the Electronics Systems Lab with Jorge Rodriguez '60 to found SofTech, Inc., commented: "The entrepreneurial culture is absolutely central to MIT. The same mix of interests, drives, and activities that makes a [Route] 128-type environment is the very life-blood of MIT itself. No other place has the same flavor." Ross epitomized this "life-blood" quality. When SofTech was established, MIT took the exceptional step for that time of making a small direct equity investment in his ground-zero company, joining a large number of friends and associates who shared great confidence in Ross's vision.

Indeed, the challenging projects underway at most of the labs create a psychological "let-down" for their participants when the projects end. Many of the entrepreneurs indicate that they became so involved with their work on a given project that, when these projects were completed, they felt that their work, too, was completed. Several of the entrepreneurs attest that their sense of identification with their lab began to wane as the project neared completion. Only through the challenge of starting their own enterprises did they think they could recapture the feelings that they were doing something important.

Beyond the labs themselves, other activities at MIT have over the years encouraged entrepreneurship. The MIT Alumni Association undertook special efforts to encourage entrepreneurship among all MIT alumni, which will be discussed in depth later. All of these efforts have spread the word, legitimatized the activities of entrepreneurship, and produced significant results.

New policies instituted by John Preston and Lita Nelsen '64, successive Directors of MIT's Technology Licensing Office (Section 4.3), further encouraged entrepreneurship, especially by faculty and research staff. In addition to conventional technology licensing to mainly large corporations for fees, the TLO actively licenses MIT-originated technology in exchange for small amounts of founder stock in a new enterprise based on that technology. In the first year of this new practice, 1988, six new companies were born based on licensed MIT technology, with 16 firms started in the second year of policy implementation. Complete, more recent, TLO spin-off data are shown later.

3.7 A Unique Culture

History, tradition, and accelerating forces contribute over time to creating a culture. Our studies of MIT alumni entrepreneurs also draw on a series of telephone interviews with these founders. We asked them whether and how their stay at MIT had played a role in their decisions to start their own companies and, if it had, how it had done so. All agreed that MIT had encouraged them to become risk-takers. One founder sees it this way: "Let me try to give you my personal perspective about 'risk-taking.' I think it is a combination of several different factors. I knew I was not going to work for big companies when I was about to leave MIT. I would rather take the risk of failure than the risk of becoming nobody. There must be many alumni who felt the same way I did. MIT offers great mentors [professors] and more opportunities [professors' consulting/research activities] for students to test the water in establishing their own business. MIT exposes students to cutting-edge technologies and new ideas. It is probably easier to explore business potential of these new ideas and technologies as entrepreneurs. It seems to be quite natural that MIT becomes a cradle of entrepreneurs."

Respondents indicated that being at MIT encourages students to become entrepreneurs, but also facilitates their social interaction, enhances their reputations [association with MIT], and trains them to solve problems — all of which are valuable inputs to new-venture development. One surveyed alumnus stated: "I look at the MIT experience as training in problem solving. Business is a series of 'problem sets' that must be solved, so MIT is a key training ground."

Another founder says that MIT instills the entrepreneurial spirit in its graduates. "You know that lots of people [students and professors] start their own companies." Many of his classmates started businesses while still in school. This founder combined an electrical engineering degree with a management degree from the MIT Sloan School, where he learned that high risk could lead to high return. After graduation, he passed up a safer job with a large company to take a senior position in a start-up.

For several years until his recent death, Teradyne co-founder/CEO Alex d'Arbeloff taught a graduate class at MIT Sloan. Having the entrepreneur who founded and built a billion dollar high-tech company as a course instructor must have been a powerful role model for his students. Amar Bose, founder/CEO of Bose Corporation, still teaches acoustics classes at MIT, albeit now as an Emeritus faculty member. Several founders observed that enrollment at MIT led to the first time they realized they were not the "smartest person in the world." One founder felt that this teaches humility, critical to CEOs who must learn to listen to customers and to respect the opinions of their employees. On the other hand, successful completion of an MIT education instills the confidence that bright people working together can solve problems.

"It's a 'hands-on' place; if there's a problem, students are encouraged to go down to the basement, build the appropriate equipment and develop a solution," said Ray Stata '57, mentioned earlier as co-founder and long-time CEO of Analog Devices (fiscal 2010 revenues of $2.8 billion). He asserted that MIT taught him that no problem was too difficult to solve. It was just a question of how hard and how long you were willing to work. As mentioned previously, Diane Greene '78, co-founder/CEO of VMware (2010 revenues of $2 billion), had a similar attitude about solving the problems of a start-up.

Along the same lines, another founder said that, because of the research and industrial ties of the faculty, MIT students get to work on "real stuff." Students are "right in the middle of something big" — topics being argued about and worked on at that moment in the industrial world. Professors do not hesitate to work on real-world industrial and global problems. Founders point out that anyone who's at MIT for a few years knows the state of the art in his or her field. Other founders mentioned the importance of ties forged at MIT with fellow students who later become customers or co-founders. "The 'brass rat' [MIT's unique and long-time traditional graduation ring that features a beaver] opens lots of doors."

3.8 "Pushes" on Entrepreneurship

Some environmental forces affecting the "would-be" entrepreneur are the "negatives" about his or her present employer, rather than the "positives" of going into business. The uncertainties due to the ups and downs of major projects have often been cited as a source of grief, and sometimes even led to expulsion of individuals into a reluctant entrepreneurial path. The evidence suggests that a stable work environment would probably produce far fewer entrepreneurial spin-offs than one marked by some instability. For example, the entrepreneurs who emerged from one large diversified technological firm most frequently rank "changes in work assignment" as the circumstance that precipitated formation of their companies, followed by "frustration in job." One-fourth of the companies from that firm were founded during the three years that the firm suffered some contract overruns and laid off some technical people, although none of those actually laid off from this firm became entrepreneurs. The "worry about layoff" and seeing the parent firm in a terrible state are cited by many of that period's spin-offs. Even at the Draper Lab, staff was cut by about 15% through layoff and attrition after the completion of the Apollo lunar program, stimulating a number of new firms. A total of 92% of the spin-offs from the MIT Electronic Systems Lab (ESL) occurred during an eight-year period, when only 28% would have been expected if spin-offs occurred randomly over time as a function only of total employment. The large number of ESL projects completed during that period is one explanation for the "lumpiness" of new company creation.

Frustration with the non-commercial environment in the MIT labs and academic departments bothered some of the potential entrepreneurs. Margaret Hamilton, founder of Higher Order Software, exclaims: "The Draper non-profit charter was frustrating, especially if you wanted to get into something exciting. There was always the sense of living in a no-man's land." Many of the entrepreneurs wanted to market specific devices or techniques. Others had no definite products in mind but saw clear prospects for further applications of the technology or skills they had learned at their current organizations. The prospective entrepreneurs usually felt they could not exploit these possibilities at MIT labs, because the labs concentrated on developing new technology rather than finding applications for existing technology. Unfortunately for their industrial employers, many of the spin-offs from industrial companies report the same frustration, despite the not unreasonable presumption that their large-firm employers should welcome at least some of these new ideas. In Silicon Valley, too, Cooper (1986) found that 56% of the new company founders had been frustrated in their previous jobs. Yet frustration should manifest itself more reasonably with just job-changing, not company-creating, behavior. Clearly, the overall environment that promotes entrepreneurship in Greater Boston, and in Silicon Valley too, makes the new-company option an active choice if other conditions are right.

3.9 Large Companies Account for the Bulk of Employment

As we showed in Table 2.1, a substantial proportion of the total sales and employment of MIT alumni-founded companies is accounted for by relatively few but larger companies. This has always been true, as we indicate in Table 3.3 for a small selection of earlier prominent firms founded by MIT graduates. Many other companies in a wide diversity of fields could be added to this list, such as Campbell Soup; AMP — $5.5 billion in revenues when acquired by Tyco International; EG&G — acquired by Perkin-Elmer; Kota Microcircuits — acquired by Fairchild Semiconductor; and Minute Maid Corporation — acquired by Coca Cola. It is quite important to point out that we list here only the MIT alumni co-founders, omitting any other founders who lacked an MIT degree. For example, Gordon Moore is not shown here as the non-MIT co-founder of Intel, nor is David Packard shown as the non-MIT co-founder of Hewlett-Packard. Nor, as earlier indicated, is Roger Marino listed as the Northeastern University alumnus partner of Richard Egan at EMC. Furthermore, as we have also pointed out before, because of founder deaths or company mergers, many of the firms shown in Table 3.3 are conservatively omitted from the economic impact projections in our study.

In Table 3.4, we show a similar small selected list of more recently created, growing MIT alumni companies, which also may spawn giants in future years. (Owing to the young age and small size of the companies in this group, we are more likely to become aware of firms that are near MIT. Over time, we assume that most alumni-founded companies will be located outside of Massachusetts, as we demonstrated earlier in this report, and they could then be found by a later thorough survey.) The combination of large and small, old and young, and mature and rapidly growing has always characterized the mix of MIT alumni-founded enterprises.

Table 3.3.   Examples of important MIT alumni-founded companies (ordered by $ sales)*.

Company	Location	Employment (thousands)	Sales* (millions)	MIT founder	MIT class	Founded
Hewlett-Packard	Palo Alto, CA	33	$126,000	William Hewlett	1936	1939
				Charles Koch	1957	1967
Koch Industries	Wichita, KA	80	100,000	David Koch	1962	(Consolidation)
Intel Corporation	Santa Clara, CA	83	43,600	Robert Noyce	1954	1968
Raytheon Co.	Lexington, MA	75	25,183	Vannevar Bush	1916	1922
				James McDonnell	1925	1939
McDonnell Douglas (merged with Boeing in 1999)	St. Louis, MO	70	20,000	Douglas Douglas	1914	1921
EMC	Hopkinton, MA	49	17,015	Richard Egan	1963	1979
Texas Instruments	Dallas, TX	28	13,966	Cecil Green	1923	1930
Digital Equipment Corp. (acquired by Compaq/HP)	Maynard, MA	140	13,000 (1997)	Kenneth Olsen	1950	
				Harlan Anderson	1953	1957
Genentech (acquired by Roche in 2009)	San Francisco, CA	11	13,400	Robert Swanson	1970	1976
				Irwin Jacobs	1957	
Qualcomm Inc.	San Diego, CA	18	10,990	Andrew Viterbi	1957	1985
ThermoFisher	Waltham, MA	37	10,788	George Hatsopoulos	1949	1956
Synnex Corp.	Fremont, CA	8	8600	Robert Huang	1979	1980
Symantec Corp.	Cupertino, CA	17	5985	Denis Coleman	1968	1982
International Data Group (IDG)	Boston, MA	13	3160	Patrick McGovern	1959	1964
				Ray Stata	1957	
Analog Devices	Norwood, MA	9	2800	Matthew Lorber	1956	1965
E*Trade Group	New York, NY	3	2400	William Porter	1967	1991
Gillette (acquired by P&G in 2003)	Boston, MA	29	2250 (2003)	William Emery Nickerson	1876	1901

(Continued)

Table 3.3. (*Continued*)

Company	Location	Employment (thousands)	Sales* (millions)	MIT founder	MIT class	Founded
America Online	Dulles, VA	6	2420	Marc Seriff	1973	2001
Bose Corp.	Framingham, MA	8	2000?	Amar Bose	1956	1964
VMware., Inc.	Palo Alto, CA	5	2000	Diane Greene	1978	1998
				Alex d'Arbeloff	1949	
Teradyne	Boston, MA	3	1609	Nick DeWolf	1949	1960
Sepracor (acquired by DSP in October 2009)	Marlborough, MA	2	1225	Robert Bratzler	1975	1984
				Tom Leighton	1981	
				Daniel Lewin	1998	
				Preetish Nijhawan	1998	
Akamai Technologies	Cambridge, MA	1	1024	Jonathan Seelig	1998	1998
Patni Computer Systems	Mumbai and Cambridge, MA	18	700	Naren Patni	1969	1979
				Charles Zhang	1994	
Sohu.com	Beijing	5	612	Edward Roberts	1957	1996
Millennium Pharm. (acquired by Takeda in 2008)	Cambridge, MA	1	527	Eric Lander	1986	1993
				Neil Pappalardo	1961	
				Edward Roberts	1957	
				Curtis Marble	1961	
Medical Information Technology	Westwood, MA	3	459	Jerome Grossman	1962	1969
				Colin Angle	1989	
iRobot Corporation	Burlington, MA	1	401	Helen Greiner	1989	1990
The Math Works	Natick, MA	2	400	Jack Little	1978	1984

*All sales and employment data are from 2010 or the most recent year available, and are rounded off to the nearest whole number, unless otherwise indicated.

Table 3.4.   Some examples of younger, fast-growth companies founded by MIT alumni (ordered alphabetically)*.

Company	Location	Employment (thousands)	Sales* ($ millions)	MIT founder	MIT class	Founded
A123 Systems	Watertown, MA	1800	97	Ric Fulop	2006	
				Yet-Ming Chiang	1980	2001
				Noubar Afeyan	1987	
Affinova	Waltham, MA	100	30	Kamal Malek	1982	2000
AgaMatrix	Salem, NH	112	34	Sonny Vu	1996	2000
				Drew Houston	2005	
DropBox	San Francisco, CA	4	0	Arash Ferdowski	2007	2007
				Jason Kelly	2008	
				Reshma Shetty	2008	
				Austin Che	2008	
				Barry Canton	2008	
Ginkgo BioWorks	Cambridge, MA	20	1	Joey Davis	2010	2008
				Eran Egozy	1995	
Harmonix Music Systems	Cambridge, MA	200	362	Alex Rigopulos	1992	1995
				Dharmesh Shah	2006	
HubSpot	Cambridge, MA	200	16	Brian Halligan	2005	2006
				Noubar Afeyan	1987	
Joule Unlimited	Cambridge, MA	80	0	David Berry	2000	2007
				Samuel Schaevitz	2000	2001
Lilliputian Systems	Wilmington, MA	60	1	Aleks Franz		
				Noubar Afeyan	1987	
LS9, Inc.	San Francisco, CA	60	0	David Berry	2000	2005
				Ganesh Venkataraman	1989	
Momenta Pharmaceuticals	Cambridge, MA	163	117	Robert Langer	1974	2001
				Inaki Berenguer	2009	
				Andres Blank	2009	
Pixable, Inc.	New York, NY	31	0	Alberto Sheinfeld	2009	2009
				Chris Loose	2007	
				David Lucchino	2006	
Semprus Biosciences	Cambridge, MA	13	1	Robert Langer	1974	2007
				Benjamin Wang	2007	
				Erik Allen	2008	
Svaya Nanotechnologies	Sunnyvale, CA	5†	0	Kevin Krogman	2009	2008
Visible Measures	Cambridge, MA	50	3	Brian Shin	2006	2005
Zipcar	Cambridge, MA	468	186	Robin Chase	1986	2000

*All sales and employment data are from 2010 or the most recent year available, and are rounded off to the nearest whole number, unless otherwise indicated.
†Indicates previous 2006 update.

4

An Evolving MIT Internal Entrepreneurial Ecosystem

As indicated above, MIT's history and unique culture began even before its formal founding in 1861 with the stated vision of William Barton Rogers for creating an institution dedicated to useful knowledge. However, institutional elements in support of this culture, both within and surrounding MIT, were slow in coming until about 35 years ago. In 1964, when Edward Roberts started his first research project to study entrepreneurial spin-off companies from MIT labs and departments, he was able to identify many MIT spin-off companies previously formed, some of which were already quite successful (Roberts, 1991). Yet, only one subject in entrepreneurship was being taught at MIT (begun in 1961, 100 years after MIT's birth) and no student club existed to encourage potential or would-be entrepreneurs.

4.1 Alumni Initiatives: Seminars and the MIT Enterprise Forum

4.1.1 The Early Alumni Seminars

In 1969, a small volunteer group of the MIT Alumni Association organized the MIT Alumni Entrepreneurship Seminar Program, hoping to attract at least 30 New England alumni from the classes of 1953–1963 to a day-and-a-half weekend session at MIT on "Starting and Building Your Own Company." All sessions on topics such as organizing, financing, marketing, and legal issues were to be run by Greater Boston MIT alumni. When advance registration passed 300, the committee cut off enrollment (330 actually attended on October 4–5, 1969), scheduled a second seminar at MIT for six months later, and began planning a nationwide rollout. Over the next three years, the committee conducted seminars in eight cities across the United States, with Professor Roberts keynoting in every city and with local MIT alumni running all of the sessions. A total of over 3000 MIT alumni attended, the largest attendance ever generated by the MIT Alumni Association for any program before or since. As far as we know, this was the first effort by any part of MIT to promote entrepreneurial activity.

Roberts recalls that, over the years, many entrepreneurs have introduced themselves, saying they remember hearing his talks at various MIT Alumni Entrepreneurship Seminars across the country. His first meeting with Neil Pappalardo '64, with whom he later co-founded Medical Information Technology, Inc. (known as Meditech, but note that the company's initials are M, I, T — the result of having four MIT alumni co-founders plus one from Northeastern University), occurred at an early MIT alumni seminar. Our survey generated many other unexpected testimonials to the direct effects of those and similar, later seminars. Bob Metcalfe '69, the principal inventor of the Ethernet and later the founder of 3Com, a great success in the computer networking market, reports that after attending an MIT alumni luncheon on starting your own business, he resigned from Xerox's Palo Alto Research Center, returned to Boston, and established his company with two other engineers. Similarly, the founders of Applicon, now the CAD division of Schlumberger, decided to create their firm after listening to a seminar at MIT Lincoln Lab that reported on the characteristics of the previous Lincoln spin-off entrepreneurs.

The seminars stimulated a variety of responses by local MIT alumni clubs. The parent committee itself organized and distributed directories of alumni who had attended the seminars and who wished to become visible to other MIT would-be entrepreneurs. "Networking" was beginning even before the term was used for that meaning! To continue its mission of encouraging entrepreneurship by MIT alumni and others, the committee also organized and authored a book published in 1974, *How to Start Your Own Business*, edited by William Putt '59.

4.1.2 The MIT Enterprise Forum

The first significant local follow-on effort was the New York MIT Venture Clinic, still very active today, which invited early-stage entrepreneurs to present their business plans and progress in an open diagnostic session of New York MIT Alumni Club members, aimed at providing feedback and suggesting ideas for improvement to the participating entrepreneurs. A New York alumnus who was spending the year in Boston transferred the clinic idea to a group of eight MIT alumni, including one of the co-authors of this report, who were active members of the MIT Club of Boston. The resulting MIT Enterprise Forum of Cambridge flourished from its 1978 founding and still continues with its monthly entrepreneur presentations, with three panelist reviewers per company, to an actively engaged audience of 200–300 persons at each meeting. Early on, non-MIT alumni were invited to join, creating the opportunity for all relevant elements of the interested Greater Boston entrepreneurial population to commingle and become involved — lawyers, venture capitalists, angel investors, and experienced entrepreneurs, as well as "wannabes." Periodic major events, such as conferences focused upon key emerging technologies or on major issues facing start-ups and growing companies, supplemented the monthly meetings and enlarged the community. The Cambridge chapter's events calendar for January 2008 illustrates the typical scope of activities: January 9, Start-up Clinic, featuring two brand-new companies; 10, Get Smart, educational session on term sheets; 17, Concept Clinic, covering issues related to technology commercialization; 21, Special Interest Group on Software Entrepreneurship; 23, Special Interest Group on Digital Media; 24, Start Smart, educational session on Choosing the Right VC. This level of nurturing and networking must be contributing enormously to MIT (and nearby) entrepreneurship.

In 1982, the Cambridge group initiated its Start-up Clinic, following a format similar to the big monthly meeting but focused upon very early-stage entrepreneurs who might not be ready to handle a large audience presentation. That monthly Start-up session was held in an informal dinner at the MIT Faculty Club, limited to a rotating audience of 40–50 attendees. In that same year, the Cambridge Enterprise Forum organized the first entrepreneurship course offered during MIT's "open" January Independent Activities Period (IAP), "Starting and Running a High-Technology Company." Since 1989, Joe Hadzima '73, an active participant in the Cambridge Enterprise Forum and recent president and chair of the global MIT Enterprise Forum organization, has led that course. In January 2011, that continuing course drew about 200 MIT undergraduate and graduate students and staff to daily sessions for one week.

The Start-up Clinic's work with early hesitant entrepreneurs has been very rewarding to all who participate. For example, Bill Warner '80 was very discouraged and about to pull the plug on his new company, Avid Technology, until he presented at the Cambridge Startup Clinic. After attendees there kicked around and were enthusiastic about his ideas, Warner decided to continue his efforts. Avid went on to change the way that film is edited, has won an Oscar and numerous awards, and has grown to peak revenues in 2007, before the global economic collapse, of $930 million. Eric Giler, a Harvard graduate, was struggling with the beginnings of Brooktrout Technologies when he appeared at the Startup Clinic. He says that the help he received led him to key customers and employees and new ideas for forging ahead. He later presented at the regular Enterprise Forum meeting, hired a senior management team of MIT alumni, built up Brooktrout, went public, then merged with Cantata Technologies, and eventually sold out to Excel.

Stan Rich, then Chair of the MIT Enterprise Forum of Cambridge, in 1985 assembled and published materials derived from the sessions to that point in time, *Business Plans that Win $$$s: Lessons from the MIT Enterprise Forum*, to provide guidance to nascent entrepreneurs and to further stimulate entrepreneurial activities.

After the mid-1970s, local MIT alumni in other cities began to mimic the Cambridge and New York activities for new and early-stage enterprises, usually with non-MIT participants as well, sometimes co-sponsored with alumni groups of other universities, such as Cal Tech and Stanford. This movement led in 1985 to the MIT Alumni/ae Association organizing the nationwide (and now for many years global) MIT Enterprise Forum, Inc. (MITEF), numbering 28 chapters in 2011, including 10 in other countries. The national office, housed at MIT, creates frequent televised panel discussions on major trends and topics of interest to entrepreneurs. For example, the January 2004 program, "Innovation at the Interface: Technological Fusion at MIT," featuring MIT professors and serial entrepreneurs Robert Langer (biomaterials) and Rodney Brooks (robotics), had a live audience at MIT of 630, with simultaneous satellite-fed live audiences of an additional 700 in 25 cities, and many additional video copies downloaded for later replay by local chapters. As an example of the diversity of topics, the September 2008 global forum program focused upon the issues affecting female entrepreneurship. Typically, 80% of the viewing audience are not MIT alumni, indicating the manner by which the MIT Enterprise Forum is encouraging entrepreneurship all around the world by MIT alumni and many others. Antoinette Matthews, director of the national office, indicates that its 2010 telecast audience was about 6000 people, with a global total of 212 unique viewing sites participating in the four broadcasts beamed by the MITEF.

There is no way to know precisely how many companies have presented over the years, nor what successes have been fostered by MIT Enterprise Forum endeavors. Lots of well-documented anecdotes abound, including that Michael Dell presented to the Houston chapter while he was still a student at the University of Texas. (Much later, Dell addressed the Cambridge chapter when he was awarded its "Edward B. Roberts Award for Distinguished Young Entrepreneurship Achievement.") The MIT Enterprise Forum of Cambridge did an intensive job of trying to assemble its history on the occasion of its 25th anniversary in early-2003 and was able to document 234 company presentations to its regular monthly meeting from 1981 (prior years' data are lost). Trish Fleming, director of the Cambridge chapter, estimates that over the years from 1978 until now, more than 700 companies presented to and were helped by the MIT Enterprise Forum of Cambridge alone in its regular sessions or supplemental clinics. The records document a large number of later acquisitions of and public offerings by these companies. On average, about 5000 total attendees participate annually in the Cambridge meetings. Perhaps an additional 750 start-ups or more received support and assistance in the other Enterprise Forum chapters. We have no idea how many of these companies were founded by MIT alumni, MIT-related persons, or others, as today all of the chapters are open in membership to all interested participants, with or without MIT connections.

In the responses from MIT's limited 2003 alumni survey, we find indications of what aspects of MIT played a role in the entrepreneurs' founding of their companies. Table 4.1 shows just those responses that are linked to alumni activities. As we have indicated the Alumni Regional Clubs were the first MIT-related channels for presenting to alumni the series of educational seminars on starting a new company. The graduation years of those affected, as shown in the table, nicely correspond to the beginnings of the alumni entrepreneurship programs aimed at earlier graduates as described above, and their continuations in various forms in different alumni regions. Further, as documented above, these programs then led to the founding of the MIT Enterprise Forum in 1978, which, over time, grew dramatically and spread geographically, attracting participation from alumni of many classes, as well as many non-MIT participants. (The drop-off in Table 4.1 in the most recent decade merely reflects the need for more time to elapse before full impact upon recent graduates is measurable.) In recent years, current MIT students have actively attended the meetings of

Table 4.1. Alumni organization influences on alumni entrepreneurship (from limited sample only).

	Proportion who rated alumni factors as important in venture founding* (percentage)				
Graduation decade	1950s ($N = 73$)	1960s ($N = 111$)	1970s ($N = 147$)	1980s ($N = 144$)	1990s ($N = 145$)
Alumni regional clubs	5	5	3	12	3
MIT enterprise forum	7	16	15	22	9

*Respondents could check all categories that were relevant.

the MIT Enterprise Forum's Cambridge chapter, suggesting that the future impact of the Enterprise Forum is likely to come sooner and also will increase in magnitude.

4.1.3   Case Example: Brontes Technology

We end this section by describing some of the dynamics associated with Brontes Technology, an example of a successful outcome from the MIT Enterprise Forum, but clearly one that illustrates the interplay among multiple parts of the MIT entrepreneurial ecosystem, some of which we describe later in this report. The Brontes single-lens 3D imaging technology derived from MIT Deshpande Center research funding to Professor Douglas Hart '85, which the MIT TLO licensed to Brontes at its formal company start-up stage in 2003. Professor Hart was a reluctant entrepreneur who had thought the principal market application would be facial recognition for security.

"I came from an era where your job was to be a faculty member and teacher, not to spin out companies," he said. However, encouraged by the Deshpande Center's executive director, Hart attended a 2002 MIT $50K Business Plan Competition networking event and met the two graduate students who eventually became his company co-founders. They all presented their preliminary ideas to the Cambridge Enterprise Forum Concept Clinic to discuss the commercialization alternatives they were evaluating for the 3D technology. That helped them formulate their business plan for the $50K competition, where they were selected as the runner-up. As the team developed a prototype system, they explored the market opportunities and discovered a large need in dental imaging. After forming the actual spinout company, they returned to present at the Enterprise Forum Startup Clinic, and then received two rounds of seed capital, followed by venture capital funding in 2004. In 2006, Brontes was scheduling a case presentation to the regular Enterprise Forum when 3M purchased the company for $93 million.

In appraising the impact of the MIT Enterprise Forum, Trish Fleming, director of the Cambridge chapter, observes: "The VCs, the lawyers, the CEOs, the management types all got used to coming here, to learning about technology, to making connections, to finding employees, to providing mentoring to students and new start-ups through the Forum. As the MIT entrepreneurial ecosystem grew, those relationships were able to grow too." The MIT Enterprise Forum, with more than 30 years of life and now 28 chapters nationwide and worldwide, has strongly influenced the culture and entrepreneurial environment not just of MIT, Cambridge, Greater Boston, and beyond but also has had untold vast effects elsewhere, influencing MIT alumni and many others to form and build new companies.

4.2   The MIT Entrepreneurship Center

In 1990, Professor Edward Roberts '57 proposed to Lester Thurow, then Dean of the MIT Sloan School of Management, that he support the formation of an MIT-wide entrepreneurship program to serve not just MIT Sloan but the rest of MIT as well. Its goal was to educate and develop those who will create, build, and lead tomorrow's successful high-tech ventures. Roberts also planned to increase dramatically and then provide central coordination and integration of MIT entrepreneurship classes and student activities.

Although based in the Management School, the initial vision for the MIT Entrepreneurship Center was that it would work to establish cross-campus collaboration with the four other Schools of MIT, especially essential to connect the business-oriented students with the science and technology students who would likely have far more advanced technical skills and ideas. This collaboration/integration would be especially vital for generating student teams to work together on real developments proposed by the outstanding MIT faculty. Furthermore, unlike nearly all other university entrepreneurship programs at that time, which rested primarily on experience-sharing by entrepreneurs and investors, the proposed Entrepreneurship Center would follow the MIT tradition of "Mens et Manus," the Latin for "mind and hand." The E-Center would have to connect rigorous scholarly pursuit of knowledge underlying entrepreneurial success, with effective transfer of that knowledge into practice. Thus, Roberts proposed a "dual-track faculty" of "tenure-track" academics along with adjunct practitioners, linking entrepreneurial researchers with successful entrepreneurs and venture capitalists, building an ambitious teaching program accompanied by direct coaching and mentoring of student would-be entrepreneurs. As part of that plan, academic faculty whose primary thrust is entrepreneurship but whose discipline base is marketing or finance or human resources, for example, would be jointly appointed to their underlying discipline group as well as to the Technological Innovation & Entrepreneurship (TIE) faculty group at MIT Sloan, which would provide overall program coordination. Over the past 20 years, this dual-track model has been adopted by almost all of the leading business schools for organizing and managing their entrepreneurship programs.

After 20 years of growth, development, and impact, those three founding principles of the MIT Entrepreneurship Center all appear to have been critical success factors: (1) engagement across the entire campus; (2) dual-track education based on integrating entrepreneurship academics with successful entrepreneurial practitioners; and (3) heavy emphasis on real-world action-learning, mixing management students with science-technology students to work on real emerging technology opportunities.

With co-sponsorship by MIT Sloan faculty across multiple disciplines, the MIT Entrepreneurship Center was launched with an initial Advisory Board consisting of prominent MIT entrepreneurial alumni, including Amar Bose '51 of Bose Corp., Ken Germeshausen '31 of EG&G, Bernard Goldhirsh '61 of Inc. Magazine, George Hatsopoulos '49 of ThermoElectron, Patrick McGovern '59 of International Data Group, and Ken Olsen '50 of Digital Equipment Corp. At the time of founding in 1990, MIT still offered only one related class, "New Enterprises," and had only one faculty member doing research in the field.

In 1996, Kenneth Morse '68 became the first full-time Managing Director of the MIT Entrepreneurship Center, which was then given a small amount of space near the MIT Sloan classrooms. In 2009, Bill Aulet '94, a serial entrepreneur who had been serving part-time as an Entrepreneur-in-Residence, became the Managing Director, and Professor Fiona Murray was appointed as Associate Director to help coordinate the large array of academic activities of the E-Center. Filled with cubicles, desks, and filing cabinets, the physical space provided a wonderful home for housing and nurturing a wide array of entrepreneurship-related clubs and activities, with immediate access to adult coaching and guidance, including several Entrepreneurs-in-Residence in addition to the Managing Director and staff. Every now and then, those staff members have to jump in to save student-run activities from unexpected glitches in plans and/or implementation. The collaborative relationships have worked very well over the past 20 years.

Over time the MIT Entrepreneurship Center label has come to represent to many at and outside of MIT both that physical space and the broad-based MIT program of entrepreneurship education and activities. The rapidly expanding MIT entrepreneurial program has contributed to a dramatic increase in the number and ambition of classes, clubs, conferences/celebrations and the resulting breadth and depth of content and contacts that facilitate entrepreneurial behavior — some have called it a frenzy of entrepreneurship!

4.2.1   Classes

Once the Entrepreneurship Center was underway, its leaders began to create new subjects, attracted existing MIT Sloan faculty to teach them and, when authorized, recruited and hired both practitioners (Senior Lecturers) and academics (Assistant Professors and above) into the program. The sole original "New Enterprises" class was gradually expanded into two sections and then doubled again as student interest in entrepreneurship grew across the Institute. While never tabulated, the number of new companies produced by that subject's MIT alumni is very high, including as examples such companies and graduates as MAST Industries, founded by Martin Trust '58, and Genentech, co-founded by Robert Swanson '69. Jon Hirschtick '83 and his roommate Axel Bichara '88 both took "New Enterprises"; later they co-founded and sold a CAD company. Jon went on to found SolidWorks, a pioneering company later sold to Dassault.

In 1993, the first new full-time academic faculty member was hired into the Entrepreneurship Program, kicking off the dual-track design and beginning to expand course offerings. In 1994, the MIT

Sloan School launched a series of educational-career "mini-tracks" within its master's degree program. The MIT Entrepreneurship Center, collaborating closely with the school's Technological Innovation & Entrepreneurship (TIE) and Marketing faculties, created the New Product & Venture Development Track. NPVD, known by the students as the "Entrepreneurship Track," quickly became the most popular track for MIT Sloan graduate students, demonstrating in the early 1990s the strong, rapidly growing interest in entrepreneurial studies and career paths. All of these "tracks" were dropped a few years later when a major change occurred in the MBA curriculum, and not reinstated until 2006, with the birth of the far more intensive MIT Sloan Entrepreneurship & Innovation Track (to be discussed later).

Soon, additional entrepreneurship-focused tenure-track faculty were hired into various MIT Sloan groups, such as international, human resources, technology and innovation, finance, and marketing, with central coordination provided by the TIE group as earlier described. Additional senior faculty from within MIT Sloan and from other departments at MIT associated themselves with the growing entrepreneurship educational efforts. A significant number of adjunct faculty members, all successful entrepreneurs and/or venture capitalists, also were recruited to bolster the dual-track elaboration, usually as unpaid volunteers eager to share their insights and enthusiasm with the younger entrepreneurial aspirants. By 2001, the number of entrepreneurship subject offerings had grown rapidly to 21 and the number of student registrants from all departments at MIT had jumped to close to 1500. Now, in 2011, students across MIT enroll in more than 30 different entrepreneurship subjects of all sorts, not including the IAP short courses. Three-quarters of the enrollments are from MIT Sloan, with 16% from the MIT School of Engineering. During the past two semesters, over 2500 "student-seats" were occupied in 47 entrepreneurship classes.

4.2.1.1 Academic classes in entrepreneurship

Over the years, regular MIT "tenure track" faculty members have developed and taught several new subjects, focusing upon their own PhD training and scholarly research. These classes include such

titles as "Designing & Leading the Entrepreneurial Organization";
"Entrepreneurial Finance"; "Managing TIE"; "Corporate Entrepreneurship"; "The Software Business"; "Strategic Decision-Making
in the Biomedical Business"; "Entrepreneurship Without Borders";
and "Competition in Telecommunications." Each of these subjects
provides an underlying disciplinary basis for entrepreneurial actions in
a given area. Other subjects also fall into this category.

4.2.1.2   Practitioner classes in entrepreneurship

Many of the new subjects that have been developed depend entirely
upon the experience of successful entrepreneurs and venture capitalists. These expert practitioners share their real-world insights, built
up over years of work, in aspects of entrepreneurship that lack much
academic theory. Some of the subjects taught by our extensive part-
time practitioner faculty members include: "New Enterprises," the
first course previously described that lays the groundwork for business plan development for new companies; "Technology Sales and Sales
Management," "Early Stage Capital"; and "CEOs at the Crossroads."
"Social Entrepreneurship" and "Developmental Entrepreneurship" are
two practitioner-based subjects that parallel "New Enterprises," but
with a focus, respectively, upon the firm that is motivated by social
problem-solving or within the context of developing countries. Other
subjects also fall into this category.

4.2.1.3   Integrating the academicians with the practitioners

As indicated earlier, the educational goal from the outset was to implement "dual-track" classes, where the students would benefit from being
taught by well-trained academics co-teaching with well-experienced
practitioners. That has taken longer to accomplish than initially imag-
ined. In the past several years those combinations have begun to take
place throughout the Entrepreneurship Program. Now, many of the
subjects listed above as either originally Academic or Practitioner are
being co-taught by both kinds of faculty members. Not surprisingly,
both types of faculty are already learning from each other, and, of
course, the students are learning from both.

4.2.1.4 Mixed-team project classes

No doubt both the theory and practice-oriented subjects in entrepreneurship, and now the integrated ones, have had great influence on their students, as we have discussed. However, intuitively, we feel that the strongest impacts have derived from a cluster of project-oriented efforts, the third broad category of subjects that we have created over the years since the MIT Entrepreneurship Program began. In these classes, the students organize in teams of four or five, preferably including participants from both management and science and engineering, to tackle real problems in real entrepreneurial organizations. Three subjects are the prototypes for the entrepreneurship program's base in this domain, what today is popularly called "action learning" and is sweeping business school education. In our case, we seem to be adding to the entrepreneurship curriculum one or more new subjects of this type every year.

4.2.1.5 E-Lab

Our earliest mixed-team "action-learning" subject was "Entrepreneurship Laboratory," or E-Lab, as it is well known. Students select from the problems presented by companies that are usually quite young (less than five years), small (fewer than 50 employees), and in the Greater Boston area, although we have violated the distance constraint on many occasions. The intent is to work on "a problem that keeps the CEO up late at night!" With the emerging company CEO as the "client," the team devotes heavy time for the duration of a semester working on her or his issue, with class time spent on communicating general principles of team management, project analysis, client relationships, some commonly used tools of market research, and in sharing reports of ongoing progress with each other. The students learn much about teamwork and the issues facing early-stage technology-based companies. Summer internships and later full time jobs often result from the E-Lab projects. By the way, local entrepreneurs volunteer far more company projects than we can accommodate in a single class, indicating the strength of the local entrepreneurial network. Frequently, the company CEOs are alumni who want in some way to "pay back" their alma mater or just to maintain contacts with MIT.

4.2.1.6   G-Lab

Two innovative entrepreneurship faculty members, Professors Richard Locke and Simon Johnson, who had been teaching "Entrepreneurship Without Borders," our subject that covers the issues of establishing new companies outside of the United States, developed an approach for globalizing E-Lab. They introduced "Global Entrepreneurship Laboratory," or G-Lab, in 2000, with the instructional and preparatory parts of the class, including team and company selection, taking place during the latter half of the Fall Term. During November and December, each newly self-organized team works with the management of its selected company, to define precise, deliverable objectives and to begin substantial background research while on campus. Then, during MIT's "open" January IAP, the teams go off to every part of the world to work with their chosen companies in three weeks "team internship" projects. Finishing the projects and evaluation by both company and class occur during February and March. This global entrepreneurial subject has rapidly grown to be the most popular elective course in the MIT Sloan School, passing 100 students in 2004 and now, for several years, close to half of the MBA class participating, providing them with a non-US entrepreneurial work experience. In 10 years, 299 host companies (23 of them more than once) in 50 countries have "employed" nearly 1400 MIT students in G-Lab projects, including 160 students during the past year. Professor Locke, who co-created and ran G-Lab for several years, says "Only at MIT Sloan could we move from brainstorming to in-the-field implementation in a few short months. The student teams have offered exciting, imaginative and — perhaps most important — effective changes in the ways that start-ups around the globe conduct business."

4.2.1.7   i-Teams

The third mixed-team real-world project class is "Innovation Teams," or i-Teams (everything must have a short name!), a "hands-on" action-learning course focused upon developing robust commercial evaluation and detailed commercialization plans for carefully selected MIT faculty research projects. The idea was conceived at the time MIT launched the Deshpande Center for Technological Innovation (to be discussed later) in the School of Engineering, which emphasized small amounts of funding for "proof of concept" research. To complement this research thrust, the i-Teams subject, operated collaboratively by the MIT Entrepreneurship Center and the Deshpande Center, leads student teams of business and technical students through the process of commercial evaluation and helps them explore the broader intricacies of the commercialization ecosystem. This includes instructing and helping each team to understand the key features of its project's underlying technology, to learn about the intellectual property issues with assistance from the MIT TLO, to scan the potential markets, during which it interviews prospective customers and industry experts, with input from the MIT Industrial Liaison Program, and to perform a go-to-market analysis. The final team report includes a recommended course of action (e.g., start-up, partnership, licensing to industry, further research in the lab), as well as key next technical, market, and commercial milestones. The faculty Principal Investigator, or one of her or his senior graduate students, works closely with the student team. A seasoned entrepreneur from the Greater Boston area, called a Catalyst, to emphasize the expectations of that person's role, coaches every team. The subject is taught in both semesters, with new projects addressed each time. In the Spring Term 2011, for example, 50 students from across MIT worked on nine faculty-initiated projects, ranging from biocompatible adhesives to geothermal drilling.

The i-Teams class was first taught as a Special Studies course by Ken Zolot '95, in response to a request to help a student-initiated project. i-Teams has since then been developed significantly in structure, academic rigor, and scope by MIT Sloan Professor Fiona Murray, working with CSAIL Lecturer Luis Perez-Breva '07 and MIT Sloan Senior Lecturer Noubar Afeyan '87. It has caught on with many students and faculty across MIT. New variations of i-Teams, with other parts of MIT, have been encouraged by E-Center leadership and achieved. In collaboration with Professor Alex Pentland '82 of the MIT

Media Lab, "Digital Innovations" was created as a mixed-team projects course to develop and experiment with extensions and uses of mobile devices. That subject has now been renamed "Media Ventures." The Media Lab itself then followed with two more similar and continuing offerings — "Development Ventures," focused upon software applications of any electronic communications or computing device to the issues faced in developing countries, and "Imaging Ventures," a mixed-team project class for conceiving and planning businesses based upon all types of visible media.

In 2008, Bill Aulet of the Entrepreneurship Center started "Energy Ventures" as another mixed-team, real-world projects subject to encourage the growing student interest in entrepreneurship based upon sustainable technologies, with energy ideas and new technologies coming from MIT faculty laboratories and graduate students. In parallel, a coordinated academic subject called "Energy Strategies" was launched to enable students to build a thorough understanding of energy markets, technologies, competition, and regulatory aspects. "Strategies" and "Ventures" have back-to-back class schedules in the same classroom, so students can do the theory and the practice together. The chosen classroom is in the center of the MIT campus, in a School of Engineering building, to help ensure that a strong group of technology-educated graduate students is enrolled to work with their MIT Sloan counterparts. One other discovery over the years is that having multiple department course numbers for each of these mixed-team subjects eases the possible problems of cross-department registration, even in such an open campus as MIT!

At about the same time as the start of "Energy Ventures," the i-Teams model was applied in a new subject called "The X-Prize," to bring into a campus-level pursuit of entrepreneurial beginnings the excitement of competing in the national X-Prize efforts to solve major problems. The MIT Neurosciences Department recently created a similar subject, "Neuro-Technology Ventures," with the same format as i-Teams. And in 2010, the latest i-Teams variant was created by E-Center collaboration with Professor Tim Berners-Lee, the inventor of the World Wide Web. His class, "Linked-Data Ventures," enrolled MIT Sloan, electrical engineering, computer science, and other MIT science-technology graduate students, and had them self-organize into mixed teams that worked on projects aimed at new business possibilities in the semantic web and in linked-data systems.

All of these classes involve mixed business–technical student teams in commercialization planning and implementation for state-of-the-art technologies. The rapid proliferation of these classes has accomplished significant cross-campus collaborative team formation around emerging technology, among other consequences becoming enhanced feeding grounds for team business plan proposals for the MIT $100 K Competition.

4.2.1.8 Other entrepreneurship classes

A number of short courses relating to entrepreneurship are offered during MIT's January IAP. For example, in 2011, one IAP course, "Starting and Building the High Technology Firm," brought about 200 students, mostly from science and engineering, daily for one week into the MIT Sloan Wong Auditorium. A few years ago we started our first entrepreneurship class restricted to undergraduates. Undergraduate education in commercialization and entrepreneurship is an area of high potential impact that requires additional faculty resources to tackle properly.

In 1998, the Entrepreneurship Center launched an intensive one-week Executive Education course, "Entrepreneurial Development Program" (EDP), taught annually during the last week of January. This program was created to quickly and efficiently increase the skills of aspiring entrepreneurs globally. In addition to aiming at ambitious individual entrepreneurs, EDP also seeks to assist government development agencies that are trying to encourage and educate promising entrepreneurs from their own regions. National and regional governments sponsor from one to a dozen carefully selected candidates each year as part of their own investments in entrepreneurial growth. EDP exposes the typically mid-career managers, nascent or early-stage entrepreneurs, to all aspects of starting and growing a company. The week includes lectures from MIT entrepreneurship academic and practitioner faculty, talks by local entrepreneurs and investors, team activities in business plan development, as well as visits with nearby emerging companies in different fields. A total of 130 students from over 30 regions throughout the world fill the MIT Sloan School's largest classroom every year for not only education but also to engage in a vibrant dialogue on the current best practices for global entrepreneurship.

Our most recent educational offering (Spring, 2011) is a unique series of eight weekly seminar sessions aimed exclusively at MIT faculty, to enhance their understandings and capabilities in the areas of commercialization and entrepreneurship of MIT discoveries. This was initiated by the interests of MIT's President, Susan Hockfield, and its Vice President of Sponsored Research, Claude Canizares, to help celebrate MIT's 150th anniversary with strengthened commitment to MIT's *"Mens et Manus"* theme. Each class includes panels of experienced entrepreneurial faculty and relevant outsiders to help elaborate the specific topic of the session (e.g., licensing technology from MIT, moving ideas toward proof of concept, financing an MIT start-up). The class size is intentionally restricted, and additional similar programs for faculty are in planning for future years.

The entrepreneurship education boom at MIT is continuing and accelerating, exposing more and more "students," at all levels, to the examples and lessons underlying new company creation and development.

4.2.2   Case Example: SaafWater

During i-Teams' tenure, some of the varied companies that already have emerged following the teams' class assistance are Avanti Titanium, Eta Systems, Hydrophobic Nanomaterials, Lantos, Myomo, SaafWater, Vertica Systems, and Viztu. Myoma is discussed in the later section on the Deshpande Center. One of the other projects, SaafWater, has built upon the research work of Amy Smith '84, Senior Lecturer and recipient of a MacArthur Fellowship, who created MIT's Development Lab program for carrying forward engineering design and devising appropriate technologies for developing countries. The Deshpande Center had funded Amy's hiring of Sarah Bird '03 to advance the phase-change incubator research project that would indicate the level of bacterial contamination in village wells. The i-Teams student group developed detailed insights to possible distribution channels worldwide and assisted the principal researchers to enter the 2007 $100K competition. The project reached the finals of the then new Development Track of the $100K and attracted venture capital investment. SaafWater was quickly incorporated and has been operating its first pilot plant in Pakistan since June 2007.

4.2.3   Clubs

4.2.3.1   From $10K to $100K and beyond

The premier student entrepreneurship organization at the outset of the MIT E-Center's existence was the $10K Business Plan Competition, created in 1990 by the MIT Entrepreneurs Club (largely engineers) and the MIT Sloan School's New Ventures Association. The original and continuing purpose of the $10K was to encourage students and researchers in the MIT community to act on their talents, ideas, and energy to create tomorrow's leading firms. A total of 54 teams competed in the first competition; the winner received $10,000 and the two runners up received $3000 and $2000, respectively. As an illustration of the MIT entrepreneurial ecosystem at work even in these early days, the finals that first year were conducted as one of the monthly programs of the MIT Enterprise Forum of Cambridge! That practice continued for 10 years as the Cambridge Enterprise Forum had the only large audience and community linked to entrepreneurship on the MIT campus. An early achievement of the new E-Center was to secure several years of funding of the grand prize from a generous MIT alumnus venture capitalist, David Morgenthaler '40. His gift freed up the students' time and energies for building the scale and quality of the $10K competition. With rapid growth occurring, the activity further benefited in 1996 by the memorial gift from the family of the late Robert Goldberg '65, which elevated the competition to become the $50K, with $30,000 going to the first place winner and two $10,000 prizes to the runners up.

In spring 2006, the then $50K competition incorporated under its umbrella the Entrepreneurship for Development Competition (plans for new businesses aimed at solving socio-economic problems in developing countries). That action inspired the student organizers to re-brand its title to become the MIT $100K, offered two grand-prize winners $30,000 each and the four runners up $10,000 each.

Undergraduate and graduate students from all five MIT Schools and 27 departments and labs have successfully entered the MIT business plan competitions over its 20 years. Figure 4.1 shows the sources of entrants to the competitions over these years, with MIT Engineering and MIT Sloan accounting for the majority. Students from Harvard and other local schools, as well as non-students, participate; however, each team must include at least one MIT student or post-doc. Multidisciplinary teams of technical and business students have proven to be the most successful competitors. These teams bring together the skills necessary for making the bridge between technology and the marketplace, the same lesson taught in a variety of the classes, clubs, and programs throughout the MIT entrepreneurial ecosystem. Panels of experienced entrepreneurs, venture capitalists, and legal professionals judge the business plans.

Tracking the transformation of competing teams into eventual alumni companies has been one of the $100K organization's greatest challenges, even in terms of how many teams competed during the early years, who were their members, but especially what happened to them following the competition. We now know that more than 2300

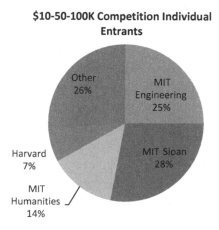

Fig. 4.1 MIT $10–50–100K competition individual entrants.

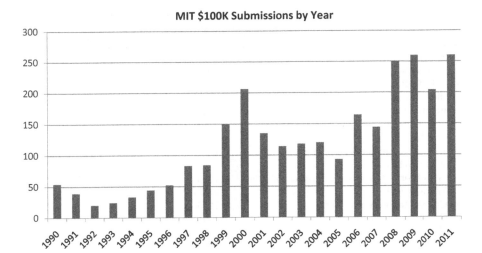

Fig. 4.2 Teams entered into the MIT $10–50–100K competition.

plans have been submitted over the years by over 9000 individuals. Figure 4.2 shows the number of teams that entered the competition annually, reflecting significant growth of numbers over time but also reflecting the cyclical effects of the Internet boom and bust.

The refinement process of the competition, its network of mentors, investors, and potential partners, and the cash prizes awarded have helped many of these teams to act on their dreams, and build their own companies and fortunes. Although records are incomplete and tracking is difficult once the students are gone, Karina Drees, Lead Organizer of the $100K in 2006, and Daniel Vannoni, Managing Director of the 2010 $100K competition, were able to document 150 companies formed through the $100K process, of which 23% have already successfully exited via IPOs or acquisitions of the firms, 41% are still in business as private companies, 17% are no longer in business, and 19% have unknown status due to lack of information. Even if we assume total failure of the unknowns, the 65% (or more) of the $100K companies that have survived or been acquired provide a remarkable success story compared with non-MIT-related companies formed nationwide. The identified-and-tracked $100K companies have received more than $1.2 billion in venture capital funding and five companies raised an

Table 4.2.   Acquisition value of select MIT $100K competitors.

Company	$10–50–100K date	Value at exit ($ millions)
Silicon Spice (acquired by Broadcom)	1995	$1200
Direct Hit (acquired by Ask Jeeves)	1998	517
SmartCells (acquired by Merck)	2003	>500*
Webline (acquired by Cisco)	1996	325
Harmonix (acquired by MTV)	1995	175[†]
Brontes Technologies (acquired by 3M)	2003	95
C-Bridge Internet Solutions (acquired by Excelon)	1996	64
Mazu Networks (acquired by Riverbed Technologies)	1995	50
NetGenesis (acquired by SPSS)	1995	44
Firefly Networks (acquired by Microsoft)	1995	40
Stylus Innovation (acquired by Artisoft)	1991	13
Open Ratings (acquired by Dun & Bradstreet)	1999	10
Optiant (acquired by Logility)	2000	3

*Does not include any estimate of future royalties that would accrue from product sales.
†However, with very significant royalties ($150 million) to the company following the acquisition.

additional $454 million through offerings to the public markets. At least 31 firms have been acquired, of which the 13 for which we have figures sold for over $3.1 billion. The transaction amounts were not disclosed in the other cases.

As shown in Table 4.2 the acquisition values of those firms formed out of MIT $100K competitors with disclosed deal values. Testimony from the entrepreneurs indicates that many of the successful companies, such as SmartCells and Brontes, were based on technologies licensed from MIT. Also the founders recognized the importance of the support they received from the vast MIT entrepreneurial ecosystem, and in many cases they had found key people to commercialize their technology through the $100K efforts.

The public data of Table 4.2 document a value capture for the 13 companies of $3.1 billion. This amount alone, a dramatic underestimation of exit value of all the $100K firms due to our lack of more complete information, represents more than a 550X Return On Investment

on the historical MIT $100K budget and a $150 million per year average return over the life of the $100K student activity. At least 4600
new jobs (no doubt many more) have been created as a result of the
MIT student business plan competitions.

We also found five $100K companies that completed successful pub-
lic offerings, raising more than $450 million at the time of their IPOs.
However, by itself the one company that is still public (two of the
five were acquired post-IPO) is Akamai Technologies, which lost in the
1998 $50K competition to Direct Hit. It was a runner-up founded by
MIT faculty and students, based upon licensed MIT technology (see
Section 4.3) that had market capitalization as of February 15, 2011 of
$8 billion.

In 1998, the student leaders of the MIT organization created an
annual MIT $100K Global Start-up Workshop located in a differ-
ent country each year, in which MIT students bring the lessons they
have learned about student team-based entrepreneurship to academic
institutions from all over the world. The workshops have been held
every year since then, in Cambridge, Singapore, Spain, Australia, Italy,
China, UK, Abu Dhabi, Buenos Aires, Norway, Madrid, South Africa,
Iceland, and South Korea, heavily attended by campus representatives
seeking to replicate the MIT experiences. This student-initiated and
run effort has helped to create competitions worldwide modeled after
the MIT activities to stimulate entrepreneurship, with participants
coming from more than 70 countries. No wonder that the MIT $100K
is regarded as "the Granddaddy of university business plan competitions." And despite the Global Start-up Workshop's success in prolifer-
ating the model worldwide, *INC.* magazine says that "[the MIT $100K]
is more equal than all the others!" To illustrate, of the 2010 group of
27 semi-finalists, 15 of them went on to launch their companies, with
six of them raising a collective $6 million in institutional capital as of
mid-February 2011.

New MIT entrepreneurial endeavors that are linked to the $100K
continue to be born. In 2005 the Cambridge MIT Enterprise Forum
chapter launched its Ignite Clean Energy Business Plan Competition,
founded and chaired by two MIT alums. For the first two years nearly
all of its events were held on the MIT campus. In 2006 an alumnus

who had volunteered for that competition took the concept with him when he moved to the California Bay Area and founded the California Clean Tech Open, with the MIT Club of Northern California and the MIT Enterprise Forum of the Bay Area as the sponsors. Since 2008, these several initiatives have been bonded together into the renamed MIT Clean Energy Prize (CEP), which has worked in close collaboration with the "parent" $100K to promote energy entrepreneurship at MIT and across the United States. Supported in part by a $200,000 grand prize from the US Department of Energy and NSTAR, the major New England utility, the MIT Clean Energy Prize attracts teams from across the United States, and also serves as the Energy Track for the MIT $100K. Five additional prizes of $15,000 each are awarded to winners in different categories of energy entrepreneurship. As is the pattern in the main MIT $100K competition, teams that make it to the semifinals benefit from one-on-one mentorship from experienced industry leaders and entrepreneurs, and connect with potential funders and customers via the high press coverage of the event. In its first three years as a national undertaking, the MIT Clean Energy Prize has helped launch dozens of new clean-tech start-ups, including FloDesign, FastCAP Systems, and OSCOMP Systems. Collectively, more than 250 ideas have competed, and CEP companies have raised over $85 million in funding and created over 400 jobs.

The competition has continued to grow enormously over the past 21 years, now including cross-campus mixers to help in the early aspects of team formation, an extensive mentoring program, coaches increasingly available to the teams as they move forward through the stages of the competition, and workshop sessions covering various key aspects of business plan development. The current version of the $100K has three regular annual "stage contests" across six industry tracks: Emerging Markets, Energy, Life Sciences, Mobile, Products & Services, and Web/IT. The first stage is the Fall Term "Elevator Pitch Contest," added in 2007 to help students formulate ideas. Next, students move to the winter "Executive Summary Contest," added in 2008, where students start to form teams and write down their ideas. All competitors receive feedback on their ideas and some cash during these training rounds, as they prepare for the larger final stage "Business Plan

Contest" in the Spring Term. Major cash prizes are awarded to the top three teams in each industry track in the spring, with the grand prize winner now receiving $100,000 in cash. In 2010, the competition gave cash grants and prizes worth more than $350,000. The competition has also taken advantage of shifts in technology, adding a TWITCH (Twitter Pitch) contest in 2010 and, adapting to this theme, went to broader social media tools with the YouPitch Video Contest in 2011. All of this continuing innovation in the $100K itself has paid off. The number of teams entered into the 2011 competition was 260, a significant increase from 2010 and a record number of participants.

The most recent "spin-off" of the $100K is the MassChallenge Global Startup Competition and Accelerator, founded in 2010 by a former student organizer of the MIT Global Startup Workshop, John Harthorne '07. John took the idea and format of the $100K to the level of the Commonwealth of Massachusetts as his base of support, enlisted strong political support from the City of Boston and the Governor's office, raised $1 million in prize money, and secured mentoring help and over 22,000 square feet of office space for the finalists. Around 450 early-stage companies applied to the first competition in 2010, representing 26 countries and 24 states. Two rounds of judging narrowed the pool to 111 finalists who were granted free resources and hands-on support for three months, while they continued to compete for the prestige and funding that would impact the winning firms. In October 2010, 16 of them won $1 million dollars in total. By August 2011, the 111 finalists had raised $90 million in outside capital and employed over 500 people. In early-2011, President Obama celebrated MassChallenge as one of the top initiatives in the country for supporting start-ups, and invited MassChallenge to join the Startup America Partnership as an inaugural member. At less than two years old, MassChallenge was by far the youngest of the initiatives chosen by the President of the United States for the Partnership.

4.2.3.2 Lots of clubs

The array of clubs tied to entrepreneurship is impressive and forms a key part of the MIT entrepreneurial ecosystem. Students at all levels, from undergrad to PhD and post-doctoral, across all MIT departments, actively participate. They contribute immeasurably to creating the unique "passion for entrepreneurship" that now seems apparent throughout MIT. Many of these clubs are housed in small spaces within the MIT E-Center; others just use the mailing lists, and get advice and help there. The clubs often represent interest groups around particular areas of technology, such as the Astropreneurs Club, Energy Club, Healthcare Business Club, Mobile Media Club, NeuroTech Club, and the NanoTech and TinyTech Clubs. All of them have speaker programs with venture capitalists, MIT faculty, and related entrepreneurs helping to educate and connect the members to early-stage firms and to new ideas in their fields. Frequently the clubs organize major meetings and colloquia.

Other clubs are more focused upon stimulating entrepreneurship per se, or providing connections for prospective entrepreneurs. For example, the Sloan Entrepreneurs and Innovators organization promotes networking events within the MIT Sloan School, and with the Greater Boston community, other local MBA programs, and established Boston organizations. Among its activities is its weekly calendar of everything entrepreneurial that is happening in and around MIT. Tech Link started in 1999 as a joint venture between the MIT Sloan student Senate and the MIT Graduate Student Council to generate social interaction across school and departmental lines for personal and professional development. With 1200 members, TechLink has become one of the largest student organizations at MIT. It organizes many major events each year, including "treks" to visit early-stage companies in different technological fields. The MIT Innovation Club centers its activities on helping its members to generate new ideas and commercialize new technologies. In fall 2009, several MIT students launched the first of its kind *MIT Entrepreneurship Review* (MITER), a student-run, student-edited scholarly on-line publication that conveys entrepreneurial news and encourages in-depth analyses of the field. Loosely based on the format of university law reviews, MITER has been a facilitator of cross-campus collaboration. Approximately 60% of the editors who emerged from the competitive selection process came from the MIT Schools of

Engineering and Science and approximately 40% from the MIT Sloan School of Management.

One of the most vital and successful student activities is the Venture Capital/Private Equity Club. Evolving from a small interest group with local speakers, the group now organizes and runs two major nation-wide conferences, the MIT Venture Capital Conference in the fall and the MIT Private Equity Conference in the spring, wholly managed by MIT students. The hundreds of attendees, from the professional community as well as MIT students, make invaluable contacts for their entrepreneurial ventures as well as for recruiting opportunities.

Growing student interest in "social impact" entrepreneurship, espe-cially in developing countries, has led to the formation of Sloan Entrepreneurs in International Development (SEID), that is similar to Sloan Entrepreneurs and Innovators but focused solely upon emerging countries as the locus of entrepreneurship. The club has been facili-tated by the recent launch of the Legatum Center for Development and Entrepreneurship (to be discussed later), with its extensive fellowship program.

4.2.4 Conferences and Celebrations

In addition to facilitating the major conferences of the VC/PE Club, the Entrepreneurship Center has gone outside of MIT's bound-aries to produce several key conferences that further enhance the environment for new firm formation. The current Managing Direc-tor of the MIT E-Center, Bill Aulet, has emphasized that these often are celebrations, more than they are conferences! The most visible of these events that have occurred in Cambridge MA has been the annual so-called "Bio Bash," more formally known as the "Celebra-tion of Biotechnology in Kendall Square." At its peak, the BioBash hosted over 850 registrants, including 150 bio-company founders, CEOs or Board members. As with the many other seminars and recep-tions organized by the MIT E-Center, one key purpose is to bring together students, entrepreneurs, venture capitalists and others who will enhance networking and communications that might stimulate additional entrepreneurship. With MIT in the center of an intensive biotechnology cluster, including the MIT-related Whitehead and Broad Institutes, creating the Bio Bash was a natural opportunity. In recent years the program has started with a professional colloquium on some major topic of importance to the biotech community, providing a "legitimate" excuse for some executives to travel to Cambridge from Europe or the West Coast just for the day.

Each semester the E-Center organizes a major networking reception in the MIT Faculty Club to celebrate the broad spectrum of entrepreneurship at MIT. It began, for many years, as an event that honored the CEOs of the numerous companies that have hosted MIT student teams participating in the long-standing "E-Lab" action-learning subject, carrying out projects at nearby young companies on "issues that keep the CEO up late at night!" Over time, that CEO partying group grew much larger, with the return of many CEO E-Lab "hosts" from previous years, as well as the angel and VC investors who relate to them. In its now-expanded purpose of celebrating all entrepreneurial endeavors at MIT, this huge love-fest of entrepreneurship also brings together the leadership and key players from the Deshpande Center, the MIT Enterprise Forum (both local and global), the TLO, the Venture Mentoring Service, and the MIT Entrepreneurship Center. This elaborate networking event still convenes and honors current entrepreneurship students, entrepreneurial alumni, venture capitalists, angel investors, and active entrepreneurs from around the community. The current students are always given prominence to try to promote summer internships and permanent jobs with the heads of the high-tech companies and their many venture capital investors who regularly attend the reception. For the past several years the spring "Celebration of Entrepreneurship at MIT" has featured the award of the Adolf Monosson '48 Prize for Entrepreneurship Mentoring, given to recognize a person or group who has been outstanding over the years in nurturing and assisting young entrepreneurs.

Over several recent years, MIT had a partnership with the United Kingdom, called the Cambridge-MIT Initiative. The transfer to British universities of insights from the MIT Entrepreneurship Center and the $100K were key components of the relationship. Annually in London, the E-Center organized a black-tie networking event that drew 500 people together to build entrepreneurial ties, attendees including the student leadership and the year's winning team of the MIT $100K competition. Even the Brits were surprised at their own enthusiasm for such rousing get-togethers. Observers at any of these conferences/receptions/ parties/celebrations could see that the real benefits were in the numerous one-on-one conversations that were happening between job seekers and job providers, between enterprises looking for money and investors searching for good targets, and between those with new ideas and those with previously developed skills wanting their next chance.

The spirit of celebrating entrepreneurship per se, as well as the entrepreneurial acts and accomplishments of students and alumni, has increasingly permeated the E-Center environment. The Patrick McGovern (MIT, 1959) award has annually recognized and rewarded student leaders in entrepreneurship, and the new Howard Anderson Fellows awards provide both recognition and cash awards to graduating students who had contributed importantly to entrepreneurship while they were at MIT. *MITER* (discussed above), our new online entrepreneurship student-run journal, was formed in part to communicate with pride news about our student and alumni entrepreneurial works.

As the 2010 graduation approached, it became clear that some large number of MIT Sloan graduating MBAs were in the process of starting their own companies. Beginning in May, the E-Center attempted to gather information on the departing students' career plans and actions. By the week before Commencement, the whiteboard in the entry lobby of the E-Center had a bold "honor" list of 32 names of MBAs who already were on their way toward their own start-ups. This information was conveyed to the MIT Sloan Dean, David Schmittlein, and then informally by him to Susan Hockfield, the President of MIT. Imagine the elation and pride of all of the MIT Sloan graduates to have the Institute's President, in her Commencement address to the several thousands degree recipients and their many thousands of family and friends guests, point out how many MIT Sloan graduates were about to begin their careers post-MIT as entrepreneurs. This kind of celebration emphasizes and communicates traditions and values that feedback into the practice of entrepreneurship at and after MIT. By the way, on the day of Commencement, 40 names were on that whiteboard!

4.2.5   Impact of the MIT Entrepreneurship Center and Network

Our 2003 MIT alumni survey sought measures of MIT-related factors that influenced the founding of the new companies. In Table 4.3, we show several dimensions that directly link to Entrepreneurship Center efforts. Clearly, MIT's entrepreneurial network was seen as a critical influencing force even 50 years ago; however, its strength has grown dramatically to the point that half of the most recent entrepreneurs see the network as a key factor in the founding of their companies. Appropriately, the MIT E-Center itself and the $10K–50K–100K Business Plan Competition had essentially no perceived influence on alumni entrepreneurs until the past decade or so, when alumni have had the opportunity to engage with them. Only a few graduates of the MIT classes that preceded the founding of these two entities had become connected with the E-Center, perhaps as E-Lab company CEOs or as $100K judges. However, during their relatively short lives, both the E-Center and the $100K have jumped into prominence as influences upon those students who later became company founders. Other survey results indicate that the more recent alumni entrepreneurs, in particular, see extracurricular and social activities as accounting for the

Table 4.3.   Entrepreneurship center factors important to venture founding (from limited sample only).

Proportion who rated university factors as important in venture founding* (percentage)				
Graduation decade	1950s $(N = 73)$	1960s $(N = 111)$	1970s $(N = 147)$	1980s $(N = 144)$	1990s $(N = 145)$
MIT business plan competition	0	1	0	3	30
MIT entrepreneurship center	3	1	2	1	12
MIT's entrepreneurial network	26	25	32	40	50

*Respondents could check all categories that were relevant.

team formation of about 60% of the new firms, with an increase in the percentage of the start-up ideas also coming from networking. The growth of classes, clubs, conferences, celebrations, and their informal spin-offs has altered the internal environment of MIT relating to these entrepreneurial movements.

As a result of all this, the MIT Entrepreneurship Center has become essentially the "heartland" of the MIT entrepreneurial ecosystem. "It" broadly educates so many of the MIT students in one or more of its classes. It nurtures and advises the many entrepreneurship-related student clubs, most of which reside in its office space. And its externally-connected courses such as E-Lab, the club activities such as the $100K and the VC/PE Club, and the E-Center major network events such as its Celebration of Entrepreneurship at MIT, bring the students, alumni, and outside community together. This does not detract from the critical contributions made by the Enterprise Forum, the TLO, the VMS, and Deshpande Center, all of which are discussed in much greater depth.

Bob Metcalfe '68, Ethernet inventor, founder of 3Com, later a partner in Polaris Ventures, and now a professor at the University of Texas, is a constant observer of MIT. "It's not just that MIT's entrepreneurial environment flourishes under its institutional commitment to technology transfer. It's also that MIT includes both 'nerds' and 'suits'. Divergent life forms, yes, but necessary to and working together at MIT on entrepreneurial innovation. And what keeps MIT's entrepreneurial ecosystem accelerating is that nobody is in charge. There are at least 20 different groups at MIT competing to be THE group on entrepreneurship. All of them are winning." Testimony supporting this effect is also presented by the 2003 results shown in Table 4.4. There we see that,

Table 4.4.   MIT factors important to venture founding (from limited sample only).

Proportion who rated various MIT factors as important in venture founding* (percentage)				
Graduation decade	1950s ($N = 73$)	1960s ($N = 111$)	1970s ($N = 147$)	1980s ($N = 144$)	1990s ($N = 145$)
Students	26	24	38	50	66
Faculty	48	42	37	28	37
Research	32	32	30	26	33

*Respondents could check all categories that were relevant.

over five decades, faculty and research have been vital to new enterprise creation but more or less constant in their importance. Whereas the perceived influence of other students upon venture founding has grown enormously, to the point that it is the dominant single perceived influencing factor found in our studies. The internal network of relationships, especially student to student, has become king!

4.3   Technology Licensing Office (TLO)

The history of the MIT Technology Licensing Office traces the evolution of the MIT entrepreneurial culture and ecosystem. In 1932, the MIT Committee on Patent Policy was formed to address issues of ownership of inventions and discoveries stemming from research done at the Institute. In 1945, the Patent, Copyright and Licensing Office was established as part of the MIT Division of Sponsored Research, one of the earliest university efforts of its type in America. It became a separate entity and was renamed the TLO in 1985. The previous Patents office had been dominated by lawyers, consistent with its formal function of facilitating patent applications and executing copyright and patent licenses with industry, government agencies, and other research institutions. With the 1986 entry of John Preston as Director and Lita Nelsen '64 as Associate Director, the lawyers were ousted and the TLO dramatically reoriented toward playing a far more active role in technology transfer. In that initial TLO year, the office put together 8–10 agreements with industry and registered approximately 120 invention disclosures. The latest figures average 80–100 agreements and about 500 disclosures per year, now under Nelsen's directorship for many years. The current TLO web site describes its mission as "to benefit the public by moving results of MIT research into societal use via technology licensing, through a process that is consistent with academic principles, demonstrates a concern for the welfare of students and faculty, and conforms to the highest ethical standards." It assists MIT inventors in protecting their technology and in licensing that technology to existing companies and start-ups.

The TLO's licensees fall into three categories — well-established (large) companies, small (often local) companies, and start-ups.

Although the TLO's licenses, in numbers, divide roughly evenly into the three categories, the majority of the exclusive licenses — the ones that fulfill TLO's mission to encourage the development of truly innovative technologies requiring significant investment — go to start-up companies.

The primary reason for the TLO's strategic focus upon start-up companies has been the reluctance of large companies to invest in "university-stage" technologies, because the risk and cost of development is high and the time to market is long. In many fields (e.g., pharmaceuticals) the large companies have become dependent on new start-ups to bring university-stage technology into proven product concepts, after which the large companies license the product from the start-up or acquire the young company. However, the TLO's effectiveness in this strategy depends on venture investors' willingness to invest in early-stage technology, somewhat scarce in the years following the burst of the "dot-com" bubble and very scarce in the recent severe economic downturn. The TLO strives to maintain a "level playing field" among many venture capital firms, to attract them toward MIT start-up opportunities by communicating fairness and openness. No investor is given a favored "inside track." Fortunately, some venture capitalists and even more angel investor groups are still interested in early-stage technologies even in difficult economic times.

Beyond the real incentives to faculty of having their ideas brought to fruition and use in the real world, some faculty, graduate students, and post-docs also participate on an ongoing basis in the companies that are started with their technologies, the faculty usually as advisors or Board members, the students (once they are alumni) often as co-founders and full-time leaders of the firms.

A typical deal that TLO structures provides technology exclusivity in a clearly specified and limited field of use (to provide clear economic incentives to the licensee), a modest license fee ranging from $25,000 to $100,000, a royalty of 3–5% of the sales that arise from the licensed technology, often with a minimum annual royalty that escalates over time. If and when royalties are collected from the licensee, they are distributed (after reimbursement of TLO expenses) one-third to the inventors, and the remainder divided between the department and/or

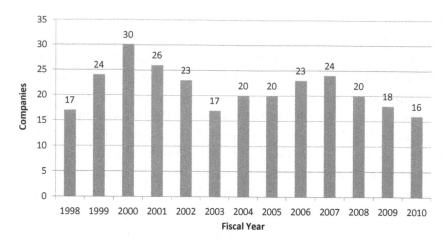

Fig. 4.3 Number of start-ups licensed by MIT TLO, 1998–2010.

center and the MIT General Fund via a formula that recovers patent expenses from unlicensed cases.

For start-ups, instead of large upfront cash payments and in lieu of some of the royalties, the TLO usually takes a small equity ownership (usually less than 5%) in the new firm. By its active engagement with faculty and other entrepreneurs as well as venture capitalists, the TLO is a vital participant in MIT's entrepreneurial ecosystem. Figure 4.3 shows the number of start-up companies TLO has licensed with MIT technology in each of the past 13 years, 1998–2010, averaging 21 new firms per annum, with some apparent (uninvestigated) cyclicality. United States university licensing data are available for many years from the Association of University Technology Managers (AUTM). Unfortunately, because of increasing external pressures for appearing to be contributing to regional and national economic development, some universities have become inventive in recent years in how they define their start-ups. One relatively new practice has been that a university incorporates by itself groups that it forms around laboratory ideas that it has patented. Besides looking good to state legislatures (and to their alumni), this practice qualifies "the start-ups" to apply for Federal SBIR and other grants that are set aside for small companies, thereby supplementing what otherwise might have to come from the university's own research funds!

Table 4.5. Primary universities
doing start-up licensing, 2009.*

University	Start-ups licensed
U. Utah	19
Cal. Tech.	18
MIT	18
U. Kentucky	14
Columbia	13
U. Colorado	11

*Compiled by the authors from
AUTM data.

Despite these new data inconsistencies, AUTM's latest survey, covering the year 2009 (AUTM, 2010), shows MIT as licensing 18 start-ups, rating it second as an individual institution only to the University of Utah. (Needless to say, MIT TLO does not "play games" with its lists of start-up license recipients.) Lita Nelsen, the TLO Director, reports that two-thirds of the way into the academic year 2011, MIT has already licensed 22 start-ups; hence, the upward recovery seems to be occurring. Table 4.5 shows all six of the US universities that licensed more than 10 start-ups during 2009. For the 178 respondents to that AUTM survey, including universities, hospitals, and research institutions, the median number of licenses per institution was just under three. The University of California system of many universities licensed 47, and the University of Texas multi-university system licensed 22 start-ups.

Over many years, MIT has usually been first among US universities in formal technology transfer to new enterprises. We do not know how many of these licenses go to companies that are not MIT alumnifounded. Nor do we know how much "leakage" might occur with unlicensed MIT technology becoming the basis for new-firm formation. Thus, the numbers cited here and in our alumni figures again inevitably understate overall entrepreneurial impact of MIT technology.

Sometimes the time required for such early-stage licensed technology to have economic impact is quite long. For example, two MIT faculty members founded Cubist Pharmaceuticals with an MIT license in 1992. After long struggles, the company has advanced to achievement of $636 million in revenues for 2010, a long haul to successfully bring new science to the market place. However, as with many companies whose original technology does not work out, during the process of growing, Cubist moved from dependence on MIT patents to products that originated elsewhere.

Beyond their formal roles, the TLO staff members, due to their organizational location and personal expertise, also actively contribute in their "spare" time to MIT classes and student activities. These include participation in sponsorship and judging of the $100K Business Plan Competition, active involvement with the MIT Enterprise Forum, and guest lectures on patents and licensing in a number of courses, both undergraduate and graduate, and clubs.

Even prior to the MIT Venture Mentoring Service (Section 5.1), which it now also helps, the TLO provided "open door coaching" for any student thinking of starting a business, whether through an MIT license or not. Several dozen students per year participate. That coaching now includes having TLO staff take on roles as project advisors and i-Team Catalysts for the Deshpande Center. All of these endeavors tie the knowledge and connections of the TLO to the rest of MIT's internal efforts at stimulating and aiding entrepreneurship. Note in Table 4.6 the increasing evidence over time of visibility and perceived impact of the TLO on venture formation, despite the fact that only a very small fraction of the alumni entrepreneurs surveyed in 2003 employed MIT-licensed technology in their new enterprises.

The influence of the TLO clearly goes well beyond the relatively few MIT faculty, staff and students who end up with patents that get licensed. A recent campus talk by Lita Nelsen, titled "Impact, not Income," provides the insights into the TLO's effects. "We

Table 4.6. Technology licensing office importance to venture founding (from limited sample only).

	Proportion rating TLO as important in venture founding* (percentage)				
Graduation decade	1950s $(N = 73)$	1960s $(N = 111)$	1970s $(N = 147)$	1980s $(N = 144)$	1990s $(N = 145)$
Technology licensing office	1	0	2	4	11

*Respondents could check all categories that were relevant.

measure ourselves by our impact on the community: New licenses (bringing innovation to the market); New products (medicine, batteries, electronic printing); New companies, new jobs; Educational exposure of students to entrepreneurial thinking and aspiration."

4.3.1 Case Example: A123 Systems

No doubt at least one interesting story can be told for each start-up the TLO licenses. A most recent one[1] illustrates both the formal and informal roles of the TLO in helping new companies to be created and MIT technology to go to market. It also again illustrates the power and workings of the overall MIT entrepreneurial ecosystem. In spring 2001, Ric Fulop '06, a serial entrepreneur (born in Venezuela), who had been involved in five start-ups by the time he was 25 years old, was looking for his next opportunity. Howard Anderson, also a serial entrepreneur who teaches the "New Enterprises" subject and several other MIT entrepreneurship classes, and was founder of the YankeeTek venture capital firm, had participated in investments in two previous Fulop ventures that had lost $10 million. However, Anderson had deep admiration for Ric and gave him space in his office next door to MIT on Memorial Drive to help Ric think through his next undertaking. After a few months of research into the energy business, and then narrowing to battery technology, Fulop scanned the country in search of technological alternatives, including reviewing the TLO's database on MIT technologies. Jack Turner, Associate Director of the TLO, discussed Ric's search with him and recommended that he meet with Professor Yet-Ming Chiang '80 (born in Taiwan). Ric described to Chiang his idea of using carbon nanotubes as a basis for setting up a new battery company. However, Chiang quickly convinced Fulop that Chiang's lab had more interesting battery R&D underway and the two of them began serious discussions. The two looked for a third partner to run engineering and Yet-Ming introduced Ric to Bart Riley, who incidentally had been an early employee of American Superconductor, an earlier MIT spin-off that Chiang had co-founded in 1987. By September 2001,

---

[1] The **A123** Story: How a Battery Company Jumpstarted its Business ... www.xconomy. com/2008/01/24/the-**a123**-story-how-a-battery-company-jumpstarted-its-business/.

Fulop, Chiang, and Riley had decided to form a new battery company, A123 Systems, and began to negotiate with the TLO (leaving Chiang out of the discussions to avoid conflict of interest) for exclusive rights to Chiang's MIT battery developments. All went smoothly with MIT and, by December 2002, the company had completed its first round of venture capital funding from Sequoia Capital, Northbridge Ventures, YankeeTek, and Desh Deshpande (born in India; see Section 5.2), who also became Chairman of the A123 Board.

The A123 story since then has been fascinating, including another round of technology licensing from MIT in 2005 of nanophosphate materials. A123 moved rapidly forward with multiple products in its three target markets for advanced, rechargeable lithium-ion batteries, including, initially, batteries for cordless tool (its first product application was the launch of a new line of professional tools by the DeWalt division of Black & Decker), multi-megawatt batteries for renewable integration into the electric grid, and batteries for transportation (with two dozen different models of hybrid and plug-in vehicles with major American, European, and Asian automakers under development). The company has raised many hundreds of millions of dollars in venture capital investments from regular venture capital firms as well as from several major corporate strategic investors, and has received numerous large incentive grants from both Federal and state governments. It went public on NASDAQ (as AONE) in September 2009, raising $380 million. It now has major manufacturing plants in Massachusetts, Michigan, China, and Korea, and more than 1800 employees. A123 has already become one of the world's leading suppliers of high-power lithium-ion batteries.

5

Recent MIT Institutional Broadening and Growth

During the past decade, four major institutional additions at MIT have contributed immediately to the development and launching of new companies, and strongly to the overall MIT entrepreneurial ecosystem. They are the VMS, the Deshpande Center for Technological Innovation, the MIT Sloan Entrepreneurship & Innovation MBA Program, and the Legatum Center for Development & Entrepreneurship, all of which we discuss below.

5.1 MIT Venture Mentoring Service (VMS)

The MIT Venture Mentoring Service was proposed in 1997 as a joint venture of the MIT Sloan and Engineering schools, with the MIT Entrepreneurship Center expected to be its host. However, as with many new ideas it took time, key people and money to actually get underway. As a result of generous donations by two MIT alumni entrepreneurs, Alexander Dingee '52 and Professor David Staelin '60, VMS finally got started in 2000, its premise being that a fledgling business is far more likely to thrive when an idea and a passionate entrepreneur are matched with proven skills and experience. In support

Table 5.1.   Some VMS Data (early-2011 report).

Ventures served since 2000	926
Entrepreneurs served	1608
Companies formed	152
Funding raised by companies	$835M+
Liquidity events (10 companies)	>$650M
Current mentor pool	148
Mentoring hours (in the past 12 months)	over 9000

of this effort, the MIT Provost gave VMS office space in MIT's main building complex, right under the MIT dome, where Sherwin Greenblatt '62, the first employee and later president of Bose Corporation, directs a small full-time staff, aided by a large number of part-time volunteers. VMS provides free, and hopefully objective, advice and assistance to anyone affiliated with MIT — student, staff, faculty, alumnus/a — who is considering the possibility of starting a new company.

As indicated in Table 5.1, in the first 11 years since VMS was founded, it has provided guidance and coaching to more than 1600 men and women participating in more than 900 contemplated ventures. Prospective entrepreneurs often come to VMS at very early stages in their idea process — usually before they have a business plan, a strategy and revenue model, a team, or any funding. About 48% of the signups are students, 40% are Boston-area alumni, and about 10% are direct inputs from MIT faculty and staff, although many of the student ventures derive from faculty research projects.

The VMS staff and volunteers do not screen to pick winners; rather the VMS mission is to use any plausible idea as the focus for education on the venture creation process. The process of forming a viable company can take anywhere from a few months to as much as five years. A total of 152 new companies, or over 16% of the ventures that have signed up as VMS "clients," had already formed operating companies by early-2011.

Ultimately, many of the prospective entrepreneurs find their ideas are not practical as ventures; however, they have learned much about being entrepreneurs and forming ventures. Some of them return with another venture concept that does turn into a company. The ventures served during the first 10 years of VMS have raised total funding significantly over $835 million. This includes venture capital and angel investments, grants, and other seed capital.

VMS's mentor pool has grown from its founding group of seven in 2000 to almost 150 mentors actively engaged in the program and working with entrepreneurs. Another 20 mentors serve as specialist resources on an ad hoc basis.

The VMS's major contributions seem to come from the "no strings attached" advice and guidance of experienced mentors. This encourages entrepreneurs to make more educated, thoughtful, and informed decisions, thereby enhancing their chances for success. Typically, VMS builds a long-term relationship that significantly influences the startup. Among the ventures that have been mentored by VMS along the path from idea to operating enterprise, showing the variety of markets and technologies being tackled, are as follows:

> *Artaic, LLC.* A Boston-based MIT spinout company that produces custom site-specific mosaic art installations, using patent-pending robotic precision manufacturing technology.
>
> *Atlas Devices, LLC.* Founded by four MIT students in 2005 to develop and field their invention: the ATLAS Powered Rope Ascender.
>
> *Brontes Technologies, Inc.* Described previously in the section on the MIT Enterprise Forum, Brontes developed and commercialized a revolutionary single lens 3D imaging technology, which it applied to the dental imaging market. Brontes was acquired by 3M in October 2006.
>
> *Corestreet, Ltd.* Infrastructure and software for security and smart credentials. Corestreet was acquired by ActivIdentity in December 2009 for ~$20M, primarily in cash but also including some stock and warrants.
>
> *Gaterocket, Inc.* Advances the Electronic Design Automation industry's ability to develop advanced FPGA semiconductors.
>
> *SmartCells, Inc.* Making use of a polymer-based dosing technology developed at MIT by one of its co-founders, SmartCells

has developed a once-a-day, self-regulating, injectable formulation for treating diabetes. In December 2010, Merck acquired SmartCells for an upfront cash payment and financial commitments of up to $500 million if various milestones are met.

VMS, its founders, and key leaders were recognized by being awarded the 2003 Presidential Citation by the MIT Alumni Association for providing an outstanding educational program for entrepreneurs at MIT. In 2007, the MIT Entrepreneurship Center awarded VMS the Adolf Monosson Prize for Entrepreneurship Mentoring, and in 2010 VMS received the NCCI Leveraging Excellence Award. Demand for its services continue to grow, with 33 new signups entering in March 2011 alone.

5.2   MIT Deshpande Center

On January 3, 2002 MIT announced the creation of the Deshpande Center for Technological Innovation, funded by a magnanimous gift of $20 million from Jaishree Deshpande and Desh Deshpande, whose most recent entrepreneurial achievement was as co-founder and chairman of Sycamore Networks. Housed in the School of Engineering, the Deshpande Center funds leading-edge faculty research on novel technologies that are believed to have high potential for commercialization. The annual award of these research funds is done uniquely by a committee of senior MIT faculty, complemented by members drawn from the New England high-technology entrepreneurial and venture capital communities. Via those linkages the thrust of the Center is to accelerate and improve the process of movement to market of emerging technologies.

Dr. Deshpande said "MIT has always provided a fertile ground where its students and faculty can break through technology barriers, fuel new areas of research and development, and fundamentally transform whole industries... Our hope... is to give creative new entrepreneurs... the ability to translate their ideas into innovative companies and products." The Center supports a wide range of fields such as biotechnology, biomedical devices, information technology, new materials, tiny tech, and energy innovations. It provides Ignition Grants of up to $50,000 each to enable exploratory experiments and proof of concept, and then provides Innovation Program Grants of up to $250,000 each to advance ideas past the "invention stage." Professor Charles Cooney '67 has served as the Center Director since the Center's founding, with Leon Sandler joining him soon after as Executive Director.

At the outset, the Deshpande Center was announced as linked to the MIT Entrepreneurship Center, most strongly evidenced by the establishment two years later of the jointly taught "Innovation Teams" (i-Teams) subject, with mixed student teams across MIT departments focusing upon developing commercialization plans for Deshpande research projects.

The Deshpande Center engages in numerous activities to seek out new faculty participants and to aid those funded to gain visibility and networking assistance from the relevant community outside of MIT. The Center has recruited experienced entrepreneurs and venture capitalists to serve as Catalysts who work closely with each research project to provide guidance about market issues and commercialization issues. Senior TLO staff work closely with the Catalysts to assist the project principal investigators, as well as to help the i-Teams that get formed around many of those projects. One of the largest Deshpande activities with several hundred enthusiasts in attendance is the annual one-day IdeaStream Symposium, featuring key MIT faculty presenters, venture capital panelists discussing the current "hot" fields, and display booths with chart sessions for all of the currently funded Deshpande grants.

From its founding in 2002 through the end of 2010, the Center has received a total of about 400 research proposals from several hundred MIT faculty. It has provided $11 million in grant funding to more than 80 projects. Follow-on research funding of the MIT projects, from both government and corporations, amounts to more than $50 million. Thus far, 23 companies have been formed, gaining over $220 million in outside capital investments, and employing more than 250 people. About 80% of those new companies have gone through the i-Teams process on their way to actual founding, indicating the strength of the mixed student teams' contributions to the actual commercialization and entrepreneurship outcomes. Professor Cooney succinctly synopsizes the Deshpande Center process as Select, Direct, and Connect: Select from among many faculty research proposals, using peer review that includes academic as well as business inputs, those that have significant promise for commercial impact; Direct the research ideas toward the market; and Connect the faculty and their research endeavors to markets and financing.

5.2.1   Case Example: Myomo

A few of the significant spinouts of the Deshpande Center are Brontes Technologies (previously described in the section on the MIT Enterprise Forum), Myomo, 1336 Technologies, Pervasis Therapeutics, Q-D Vision, Taris Biomedical, and Vertica Systems. One example of Deshpande Center commercialization is Myomo, started with Deshpande funding in 2002 as the "Active Joint Brace" research project of Professor Woodie Flowers 1968. The case again reflects the strong interrelationships of various parts of the MIT entrepreneurial ecosystem. The project's evolution from academic research toward commercialization may be seen symbolically in the descriptions of the work used at various times. The research group's initial self-description was: "Our research group aims to create a wearable, affordable, unencumbering exoskeleton that augments human physical capability by working in parallel with existing muscalature." After its first pass with an i-Teams group effort, the work was described as: "Active Joint Brace is an orthopedic joint brace combined with a powered assist mechanism modulated by a neurological sensor."

By the end of the semester with their i-Teams group, they were introducing their technology by pointing out: "Ten million of the twenty-one million Americans living with disabilities have difficulty lifting a light object such as a fork or a toothbrush." At that point in 2004, the team, consisting of MIT faculty, students, and an alumnus, plus a Harvard student, entered the $50K Business Plan Competition and won the Robert Goldberg Grand Prize of $30,000. By January 2006, the research project was finished and Myomo Inc. (short for My Own Motion) was born. In July 2007 it received FDA clearance to market its first product for partial rehabilitation of stroke victims. In November 2007, it received the *Popular Science* "Best of What's New" Award for its NeuroRobotic Technology Innovation.

As of January 2010, Myomo's current CEO, Steve Kelly, was upbeat about company prospects and acceptance of its underlying technology, but admitted to continuing struggles to raise the financial support needed to grow the company.[1]

5.3 MIT Sloan Entrepreneurship & Innovation MBA Program

Entrepreneurship & Innovation (E&I) is a new intensive "track" within the two-year MIT Sloan MBA Program, made available for the first time to selected applicants in the entering MBA Class of 2008. Professor Edward Roberts has chaired E&I from the outset, focusing the program on teaching committed graduate students how to launch and develop emerging technology companies. The E&I Track attempts to build a select lifetime cohort of collaborating entrepreneurial MBA classmates, and leads to an MIT Sloan Certificate in E&I in addition to the MBA degree. The E&I curriculum heavily emphasizes team practice linked to real-world entrepreneurial projects, balances theoretical and practitioner education, and provides a thorough exposure to the many building blocks of an entrepreneurial career. Perhaps not surprising to some, over one third of the entering MBA students applied for admission to this new opportunity when it was announced in June 2006, but the 125 had to be screened down to 50 first year students in order to manage program introduction. Over 40% of the entering MIT Sloan MBAs now enter this entrepreneurship concentration.

The E&I program begins with the standard first-semester MIT Sloan MBA core, permitting the entrepreneurship cohort to become fully integrated with their classmates in all activities. However, during that first term, the E&I participants also take an overview course that introduces them to all aspects of entrepreneurship education and practice at MIT. Both academic and practitioner faculty meet with the group, as do the heads of the MIT TLO, VMS, Deshpande Center, and several local entrepreneurs and venture capitalists, creating special

---

[1] http://www.massdevice.com/features/massdevice-qa-myomo-ceo-steve-kelly, accessed on February 26, 2011.

access to the MIT entrepreneurial ecosystem. The semester is followed soon after in the Spring Term by an intense one-week group trip to Silicon Valley arranged by the MIT E-Center. The class visits leaders of multiple venture capital firms and meets in small groups with a large number of carefully selected, early-stage high-tech firms in the life sciences, medical technology, software, information technology, media, advanced materials, and new energy fields. During their following three semesters in the MIT Sloan MBA Program, E&I participants must engage in at least one MIT $100K business plan team (described above) and choose several additional subjects from a restricted menu of entrepreneurial electives (including E-Lab, G-Lab and i-Teams, all described previously). These entrepreneurship classes help prepare them to start and build companies while letting them enroll in other broadening MIT and MIT Sloan courses such as in finance or marketing.

One of the students in the inaugural MIT Sloan E&I class, Nikhil Garg, MBA '08, described his experience: "I could have spent my entire two years on campus meeting like-minded entrepreneurs here and there. But everyone in this class wants to start a company. It's so much easier to facilitate ideas and business relationships with other MBAs and techies in this type of environment." Will O'Brien, MBA '08, spearheaded weekly 30 minutes "Open Mic" sessions to encourage his classmates to practice their pitches, preparing them for future encounters with venture capitalists. "The caliber of ideas has been phenomenal," says O'Brien. "They've ranged from new ventures in wind energy, developmental entrepreneurship, media, and even beer manufacturing." In December 2008, Will launched a Web 2.0 company that he began with an E&I classmate during their second year in the program.

Half of the inaugural group had previously founded their own or been part of start-up companies. Many more company formation initiatives began even within the first term of the students' arrival on the MIT campus. A group of the first-year E&I class demonstrated their entrepreneurial savvy by winning the UC-Berkeley School of Business "Media Case Competition," sponsored by Yahoo!, and took home a check for $10,000. Another first-year E&I participant became part of an African–American team that won the $10,000 first prize at the 2006 Whitney M. Young New Venture Competition at the Wharton

School, the three finalists being MIT, Stanford, and UCLA. One more classmate was a $1K winner and another a finalist in the MIT $100K competition.

As of March 2011, with five E&I classes underway, the evidences continue to grow of strong MBA student desires to create their own new firms. Despite the E&I program leadership's guidance that they first gather more real-world experience working in start-ups before initiating such actions on their own, more of the MIT Sloan MBA class each year are immediately kicking off their own companies. About 25 '08 MBA graduates, the first year of E&I program completion, started their companies before or upon graduation from MIT, three times the number of immediate start-ups from the Class of 2007. And, as mentioned previously, this number grew to 40 start-ups by graduation of the Class of 2010. This may be an early sign of the E&I Track's impact on its own group as well as on other entrepreneurial classmates.

5.4 Legatum Center for Development & Entrepreneurship

The Legatum Center for Development and Entrepreneurship was founded in 2007 through a structured gift of $50 million from the Legatum Group, a global investment firm. Its mission is to enhance economic progress and good governance in low-income countries through the encouragement of entrepreneurship and innovations that affect the lives of ordinary citizens. Its philosophy is to stimulate bottoms-up development, and its two primary mechanisms are an annual "Convergence" and its growing fellowship program. The Convergence brings together large numbers of global experts on aspects of entrepreneurship in emerging markets, to elaborate further the Legatum Center's theme of bottoms-up development and to communicate that message more widely.

The Center's competitive fellowship program is open to all MIT graduate students who commit themselves to attempting to create and launch a new enterprise in a low-income nation. The Center provides its Fellows with specialized small-group seminars, coaching on business plan creation, participation in the annual Legatum Convergence and other networking events, and especially the financial assistance to permit them to advance their MIT degree programs. A majority of the Fellows are enrolled in the MIT Sloan School, either as two-year MBA students or in the one-year Sloan Fellows in Innovation & Global Leadership mid-career masters degree program.

Growth in the numbers of Legatum Fellows is increasingly reflected in entries to the Development Track of the $100K competition and in the activities of the SEID club. In 2011, SEID received a grant from the National Collegiate Inventors and Innovators Alliance to develop elements of a Social Entrepreneurship Ecosystem at MIT to parallel the existing MIT for-profit ecosystem.

6

Conclusions: Enhancing the Role of Research/Technology Universities in an Entrepreneurial Economy

Universities that are strong in research and technology are at the forefront of knowledge creation and potential application. When the university is able to couple this capability with the inclination and resources needed to connect ideas and markets, impressive possibilities exist for generating entrepreneurship-based economic impact at the local, as well as national and global, levels. Most important in making this transformation is having the leadership of the institution adopt the will to accomplish this. Numerous changes are needed in most universities over an extended period of time in rules, regulations, and, more important, attitudes and institutional culture. None of these will be accomplished without strong and committed university leaders.

The MIT history described in this report provides numerous and detailed examples of how one major institution achieved significant entrepreneurial impact over its first 150 years. In synopsizing them now, we point to ways that other universities can move toward enhanced entrepreneurial effects.[1] Early examples of engaging the academic with

---

[1] In Appendix, Alumni Surveys at Other Universities, we present our current information on alumni entrepreneurship studies carried out at other universities in the United States and China.

the real world, even including entrepreneurial actions by senior and respected faculty and university officials, did much to capture the attention of more junior faculty members, as well as students and alumni, to the legitimacy of technology transfer and commercialization. Big differences between institutional histories of entrepreneurial output no doubt are explainable to a great extent by this distinction alone in leadership roles and behavior. MIT's history suggests that the appropriateness of rules and regulations needs to be assessed carefully to be sure that they do not create barriers to faculty participation in industrial consulting and, more vitally, that they do not hinder faculty initiatives in new company formation. A shift from barriers toward incentives will take much time to occur in most academic organizations and will be accelerated if advocates for entrepreneurship pay strict attention to establishing and enforcing strong guidelines against conflicts of interest.

Until quite recently, MIT had followed a "hands off" approach toward entrepreneurial engagement, in contrast with many other universities in the United States and abroad. MIT has neither created an internal incubator for ventures nor a venture capital fund to make life easier for prospective start-ups. Those facts have permitted MIT to avoid degrees of internal conflict and occasional embarrassments that have plagued other academic institutions that have tried to hurry the entrepreneurship process. However, MIT has had the advantage of a surrounding community that essentially has provided those functions, as well as other aspects of a supportive infrastructure for new enterprises. In less well-endowed neighboring circumstances, a university may have to supply with great care the active help and at least some funding to aid in getting entrepreneurial ventures off the ground.

Instead, MIT has relied internally upon growing faculty, student, and alumni initiatives, especially during the most recent 30 years, to build a vibrant ecosystem that helps foster formation and growth of new and young companies. All these have, over time, significantly enlarged the number of interested and involved participants, with corresponding increases in their activities and outcomes. If an institution deliberately tries quickly to become more entrepreneurial, the MIT approach would take an amazing degree of patience and self-restraint.

Outreach to alumni is achieved easily in the form of self-organized seminars, and faculty visits and lectures, facilitated by direct "distance viewing" of classes and conferences. Organizations such as the MIT Enterprise Forum often can be accessed in local communities, perhaps just by joining or partnering instead of needing to replicate the organization, reaching critical mass much sooner along with greater community-level interaction.

Educational programs require investment in and acquisition of faculty to develop and teach such programs. Effective and well-trained academics are unfortunately still scarce in most entrepreneurship-related disciplines. Fortunately, successful practitioners are available everyplace and the MIT history indicates that they are quite willing and enthusiastic about sharing their time and experiences with novice and would-be entrepreneurs. The list of MIT student clubs suggests the numerous ways by which students across the university might find their own paths toward entrepreneurial efforts. The $100K business plan competition is the most vibrant and perhaps most effective of these clubs on the MIT campus, leading directly to high levels of new companies being formed. Students at other universities can learn easily how to undertake their own comparable competitions through attending the annual MIT $100K Global Startup Workshop. Furthermore, the MIT one-week intensive Entrepreneurial Development Program, conducted annually in January by the MIT Entrepreneurship Center, may well be a helpful supplement for those institutions attempting to create an overall program of education and student activities that will encourage entrepreneurship. This is now being complemented by the MIT E-Center's launch in 2011 of REAP, Regional Entrepreneurship Acceleration Program, a limited membership consortium aimed at assisting regions in the United States and abroad to develop and implement ambitious programs of enhanced economic development through stimulating entrepreneurship.

The alumni activities, educational and student endeavors provide a strong basis for building an entrepreneurial ecosystem. However, formal institutional activities are also critical. At MIT, changing the TLO into a proactive and supportive-of-entrepreneurship program office has contributed much to technology transfer from the research labs. This was done 25 years ago and has had the time to mature in its effectiveness. More recently, MIT's creation of the VMS, its own form of volunteer lightweight but quite effective "incubation," has generated a model of helping that is clearly possible in many other university communities. And direct, targeted funding of faculty research that has commercial potential, as done in the new MIT Deshpande Center, is certainly a possibility elsewhere.

This report has documented how MIT alumni, students, staff, and faculty who have formed new enterprises over the past 50 years have generated so much dramatic economic impact, a large fraction of that impact strongly influenced by the transfer of knowledge and skills from MIT and other universities. Throughout, we have attempted to communicate the many elements of what we call this university's entrepreneurial ecosystem, and how each part has contributed to the venture formation process. In many examples we have cited, multiple aspects of that ecosystem have been at work in making entrepreneurship happen and be successful. We have also tried to show how other universities may be able to strengthen their own entrepreneurial achievements, and, in turn, their contributions of economic impact upon their communities, regions, and countries.

Appendix

Sources of Information[1]

A.1 Company Database

In 2003, MIT initiated a rigorous and comprehensive survey effort, in which the authors participated, to identify, carefully study, and assess

[1] *Information on MIT Entrepreneurial Organizations*: We deeply appreciate the help of many MIT faculty, staff, and alumni in the preparation of this report. In particular, Trish Fleming and Antoinette Matthews, Directors of the MIT Enterprise Forum of Cambridge and globally, respectively, along with Joseph Hadzima '73, former chair of the global Enterprise Forum organization, provided huge amounts of information from which we developed much of the detailed history of that remarkable organization. Karina Drees '07, Lead Organizer during 2006–2007 of the MIT $100K Business Plan Competition, assembled and presented much of the information in regard to the $100K; Daniel Vannoni '11, its Lead Organizer during 2010–2011, did similar work in updating that information. Lita Nelsen '64, Director for more than 25 years of the MIT Technology Licensing Office (TLO), gave us much insight to the MIT entrepreneurship process and supplied all of the data on the history and operations of TLO. Sherwin Greenblatt '62, Director, prepared the data on the MIT Venture Mentoring Service. Professor Charles Cooney '67, its Faculty Chair, and Leon Sandler, Executive Director, provided key information about the MIT Deshpande Center. Ken Zolot '95 and Professor Fiona Murray assembled the information about the related Innovation Teams class. Anurag Bajpayee '08 supplied the updated information about the MIT Global Startup Workshops. Bill Aulet '94, Managing Director of the MIT Entrepreneurship Center, and Jose Pacheco '94, its long-term Program Manager, supplied details on many aspects of operation of the E-Center and its extensive coursework and activities.

the impact of new enterprises created by all living alumni.[2] The survey produced detailed information on 4611 companies founded by 2111 graduates. To provide still more information about these companies, including current sales, employment, industry category, and location, this new MIT database was further updated and upgraded from the 2006 records of Compustat (for public companies) and Dun & Bradstreet (private companies). Our report's findings with respect to total employment and sales, MIT-enrolled department of company founders, industry, and age of companies are based on this updated database. We use data only on MIT alumni companies that still were active in 2003, that information coming from a carefully conducted survey process. In this manner, and many others, the numbers in our report are likely to be a significant underestimate of the total economic impact of MIT-*related* entrepreneurs, ignoring the entrepreneurial outcomes of the many non-alumni faculty, staff, and other employees, as well as other spillovers from MIT. We do comment on these other MIT-*related* enterprises where appropriate in the report.

A.2 Alumni Survey

MIT conducts periodic surveys of all alumni,[3] approximately each decade, to get up-to-date demographic information. As we indicated previously in this report, in 2001 MIT sent a survey to all 105,928

We also thank William Bonvilian, head of MIT's Washington DC office, for his help in acquiring the resources needed for carrying out the analyses. Lesa Mitchell, Vice President of the Kauffman Foundation, was instrumental in getting the report published, along with many others from Kauffman, to whom we are ever grateful.

Additional Thanks: Celia Chen, Jennifer Peterson, Minnie Moy, and Yuqiao Huang made important contributions to the data analyses and presentations in this report. We are grateful for their assistance and hard work. Of course, any errors are the responsibilities of the authors.

[2] About 10 years before, the Economics Department of BankBoston (now part of Bank of America) collaborated with some MIT staff members on an analysis of MIT-related companies. The 1997 publication by BankBoston used information on some number of then-active MIT-related companies that had been identified as created by MIT faculty, staff, and employees of MIT-affiliated research labs.

[3] The term "alumni" includes both male alumni and female alumnae. Furthermore, "alumni" are defined by the MIT Alumni/ae Association to include all persons who received an "earned" degree from MIT, as well as those who were registered in a degree-granting program for at least one full undergraduate term or two full graduate terms.

presumed living alumni with addresses on record. MIT received 43,668 responses from alumni; of these, 34,846 answered the question about whether or not they had been entrepreneurs. A total of 8179 individuals (23.5% of the respondents) indicated that they had founded at least one company. In 2003, we developed and sent a survey instrument that focused on the formation and operation of their firms to the 8044 entrepreneur respondents for whom we had complete addresses. Of the 2111 founders who completed surveys, approximately 2.2% of the cases had been reported by more than one MIT co-founder. Removing those duplicates (the average number of MIT co-founders per team is 1.29) left 2059 unique alumni entrepreneur respondents who founded 4611 companies. Most teams also had non-MIT co-founders; however, this fact does not require any correction in the sample.

Because many of the founders of the largest MIT alumni companies no longer are affiliated with their companies or have passed away, the companies represented in the survey responses are somewhat more recent and average fewer employees than the universe of MIT alumni-founded companies. All told, these 4611 specific surveyed firms included in the direct responses employ more than 585,000 people. We estimate, however, that the entire population of MIT alumni firms employs more than 3.3 million people.

The report's findings on where and why companies locate where they do, what gives them their competitive edge, how they received initial funding, where they sell their products, and how many patents they have are taken directly from the responses to this 2003 survey, updated to reflect the 2006 corporate information obtained from Compustat and Dun & Bradstreet. However, to estimate accurately the entrepreneurial activity and economic impact of those in the entire MIT alumni population who did not respond to the surveys, we multiply the direct response numbers by a scale factor. For further details, see Section A.4.

The detailed questionnaire used for this survey is available at www.kauffman.org/MITstudy. We encourage other universities to undertake and share comparative analyses. We discuss in the following section some alumni entrepreneurship studies that have both preceded and followed our efforts at MIT. We should note here that although we correctly identify all of the alumni in the MIT database as "MIT alumni," a substantial fraction of them are also alumni of other universities in the United States and other countries. Hence, the economic impacts cited in this report reflect the direct and indirect educational impact of many institutions of higher learning in science, technology, and management.

A.3   Alumni Surveys at Other Universities

It may be helpful to look at other university alumni surveys that have focused upon entrepreneurship. However, given differences in survey methodology and the way alumni were asked about entrepreneurship, results across surveys cannot readily be compared. Ron Burt (2001) collected a survey of alumnae of the University of Chicago Graduate School of Business in 2000. A total of 800 alumni responded to the survey and the authors used both a second-wave non-respondent survey of 1000 non-respondents and the school's alumnae database to check for non-response bias. The only bias detected was that women no longer in the labor market (retirees and housewives) were less likely to respond to the survey. Burt uses the survey to ask questions about how women use their personal and professional networks.

In 1997 William Barnett and Stanislov Dobrev (2005) surveyed the alumni of the Stanford University Graduate School of Business. They received 5283 completed (or partially completed) surveys for a response rate of 43%.[4] The data set includes general demographics, career histories, including job changes, the features of previous job positions and the organizations where they were employed. The authors used interpolation where possible to handle missing values and excluded the rest of the surveys. By this method, only 2692 surveys were complete. The authors examined the distribution of basic demographic characteristics between the full sample and the final sample after excluding missing cases and found no detectable bias. However, it is still unclear whether there is bias between the final sample and the underlying population.

---

[4] Lazear (2004) notes that the response rate may have been even higher if one takes into account that some individuals were very old and others may no longer have been alive to receive the surveys.

Their theory and data distinguish between self-employment and founding a new organization. One advantage of the Barnett–Dobrev data set is the ability to observe a wide range of entrepreneurial firm ages. This wide variance was important for their questions about how demands from the environment and work roles shift as organizations grow and age. The mean firm age was 7.4 years and the mean employee size was 468.

Edward Lazear (2004) used this same data set to ask whether entrepreneurs tend to be generalists or specialists by matching the data with student transcripts and looking at the pattern of their MBA coursework and career history. Dobrev (2005) also uses these data to ask whether there appears to be evidence for social "flocking" behavior in choosing careers in finance or consulting.

Joshua Lerner (2009) used Harvard Business School "class cards" that students complete on matriculation to provide data on 6000 HBS students and the sections that they are in. The students received a survey at graduation where they were asked to indicate the jobs that they are entering, including entrepreneurship. The authors used these data to determine whether being in a section at HBS with former entrepreneurs influenced the likelihood that graduates would become entrepreneurs in their initial jobs after graduation. They find that having entrepreneurial classmates actually deters potential entrepreneurs; however, it appears to be true for those HBS alumni who were most likely expected to fail had they become entrepreneurs. The results indicate a type of screening mechanism for bad business ideas.

William Baumol has conducted a pilot survey of the current undergraduate seniors, current MBA students along with MBA and undergraduate alumni of five US universities, to be expanded to include universities overseas in a subsequent round of surveys (Summit Consulting, 2009). The initial responses come from 4731 current senior undergraduate students, 431 current MBA students, 283 undergraduate alumni (Class of 2000), and 153 MBA alumni (Class of 2000). Response rates were good (23.6–30.6%) for most groups, except only 6.0% for the undergraduate alumni. The survey title mentions entrepreneurship and correspondingly entrepreneurs appear to have been significantly more likely to respond to the survey, making it difficult for this round of the survey to estimate accurately the impact of entrepreneurship courses on rates of alumni entrepreneurship. The study focuses on educational curriculum and experiences and the impact on the subsequent choice of entrepreneurial careers and whether the individuals engaged in innovative or replicative entrepreneurship. Preliminary results show that, even when controlling for parents' entrepreneurship, students who took entrepreneurship courses were more likely to become entrepreneurs and were more confident in their entrepreneurial skills. Results appear to suggest that those who took entrepreneurship courses were more likely to be innovative entrepreneurs. However, most of the respondents who took entrepreneurship courses were MBA alumni who also had higher opportunity costs; hence, replicative entrepreneurship might have been less likely due to the higher education level and opportunity costs of this sub-group. Causal inferences are not possible at this stage. Overall the survey focuses on a large number of questions detailing the character and type of educational experiences and assignments the individual had while in school.

Jolly et al. (2009) conducted an alumni survey of Iowa State University alumni.[5] They used a proportional random sample and sent surveys to 25,025 alumni (only Bachelor's degree recipients) and received 5416 responses. They find that 16% of the alumni have started businesses, mostly in Iowa. In addition, they asked questions about geographic location, careers, income, community service, family life, and founding non-profit organizations as well.

Both of this report's co-authors collaborated with Prof. Delin Yang of Tsinghua University in Beijing to launch in 2007 what to the best of our knowledge was the first alumni entrepreneurship survey outside of the United States. The survey was based on the MIT survey, but tailored to the Chinese context and translated into Mandarin. The survey was sent to all alumni with address on record (a total of 26,700) who graduated between 1947 and 2007. Alumni were asked if they participated in founding a new company or separately about privatizing a state-owned enterprise. A total of 2966 surveys have been received

---

[5] The Iowa State summary report is available here: http://www.econ.iastate.edu/research/webpapers/paper_13031_09002.pdf.

online and via paper and e-mail (including 718 entrepreneurs). This database represents, to our knowledge, the first large-scale database of technology-based ventures in China. Applying the same methodology used in our MIT study, we estimate that 13,600 firms have been created by Tsinghua alumni. These firms have generated 633 billion RMB in worldwide revenues (50 billion USD) and employ 8.1 million people in the aggregate. The total GDP would be the equivalent of half of the city of Beijing and would total the 70th largest country (larger than Luxembourg). However, it is important to note that entrepreneurship has a much shorter recent history in the Chinese context; hence, the average age of the Tsinghua firms is significantly lower than the MIT alumni firms.

A number of other universities have inquired about using the MIT questionnaire for their alumni surveys. As indicated above, our detailed questionnaire is available at www.kauffman.org/MITstudy. While we are not aware of the results of these inquiries, similar survey efforts have been considered at a number of schools, including Hong Kong University of Science and Technology, Instituto de Empresa Business School in Madrid, Technion Israel Institute of Technology, Universidad Catolica in Chile, Universidad de los Andes in Colombia, and the University of Southern California. In April 2011, Prof. Ethan Mollick of the University of Pennsylvania sent a career survey to the Wharton MBA alumni. The data from that survey are still being compiled and no results are available yet.

In May 2011, one of this report's co-authors has launched a comprehensive study of Stanford University alumni/ae. This survey was sent to approximately 140,000 Stanford alumni/ae across graduation years. Current faculty and research staff were also included. In addition to gathering information from alumni about their careers and innovations, alumni were asked whether they had founded non-profits or played a number of possible key roles in entrepreneurial firms. Specifically, the survey asked follow-up questions not only of the entrepreneurs, but also of those who identified themselves as having been early employees (joining within the first year), Board members in private companies, angel investors and venture capital investors. This survey should provide a relatively more complete picture of the group of individuals involved in creating entrepreneurial firms. The data collection phase is still ongoing and results should be available in the coming months.[6]

One of the report's co-authors has also been advising a similar alumni entrepreneurship survey effort at the University of Virginia (UVA) by Prof. Michael Lenox of the Batten Institute. Our hope is eventually to create a combined data set that would enable systematic analysis of university level policies and programs over time. The UVA survey will be launched in the coming weeks. The Stanford and UVA survey instruments were based on the MIT survey with some overlapping questions to enable comparison and some new questions as well. The Stanford survey questionnaire will also be made publicly available. We hope that other universities will use a similar version of the survey and methodology to enable more direct future benchmarking and analysis across universities. Given the growing interest in alumni surveys as a methodology in entrepreneurship research, one of this report's co-authors has written a separate paper on the use of alumni surveys in entrepreneurship, the types of questions appropriate to them, their limitations, and mythological issues as well as suggestions (Eesley, 2011).

A.4   Estimation Methods

As in all surveys, a large segment of the alumni population did not respond to the MIT alumni surveys. Therefore, estimation of the total impact of MIT alumni entrepreneurs requires extrapolation to account for the non-respondents. To estimate the numbers for the entire MIT alumni population, we multiply by a scale factor to give an accurate estimate of the entrepreneurial activity of those who did not respond. As we have aggregated data from both the 2001 and 2003 MIT surveys, with adjustments from the 2006 Compustat and Dun & Bradstreet databases, the appropriate scale factor depends on the particular statistic or question being answered.

1. For survey items where we have data on all companies created over the life of the entrepreneur, the base scale factor

---

[6] For the interested reader, weekly updates on the response rate and initial analysis are available at http://stanfordinnovationsurvey.blogspot.com.

is approximately 9.476 (i.e., $2.425 \times 3.906 = \sim 9.476$). These numbers are approximate since we actually use more than 3 digits after the decimal. We multiply by 2.425 because, as indicated above, the total population of MIT alumni is 105,928 and 43,668 responded to the first survey. To get from 43,668 to 105,928 we have to multiply by 2.425 (i.e., $105,928/43,668 = \sim 2.425$). Then we multiply by 3.906 since 8044 indicated that they were entrepreneurs and only 2059 responded to the Founder's Survey (i.e., $8044/2059 = \sim 3.906$). We multiply that by 0.773 to avoid duplicate counting by correcting for multiple MIT alumni on the same founding teams. Because 23.4% of the reported companies were out of business by 2003, we finally multiply by 0.766 to count just those companies likely to still be active.

2. For items where we only have data on one of the companies the entrepreneur founded, we then multiply by 1.61 since 1.61 is the number of companies on average each entrepreneur has founded (27% of the entrepreneurial alumni are repeat/serial entrepreneurs). For example, if we take 100 alumni entrepreneurs, on average they would have created 161 companies during their careers. If we only have data on total employees for one company each (100 companies), then we must multiple by 1.61 to get an estimate of the real total number of employees for all the companies created by that entrepreneur.

3. We further adjust the scaling factor for items where data are missing due to entrepreneurs skipping a survey item. This process may seem complicated; however, it gives a much more accurate estimate than any previous efforts.[7]

It is important to point out that although we correctly identify many different MIT alumni-founded companies in various discussions

---

[7] Similar extrapolation methods were used in a recent study of immigrant entrepreneurs' role, using a scale factor to extrapolate from 2054 responses in their survey database to the estimated economic impact drawn from 28,776 companies, a scale-up factor of ~ 14.010 (Wadhwa et al., 2007).

throughout this report (e.g., Tables 3.3 and 3.4), in the underlying database that gets scaled we only use those firms formed by alumni who completed survey reports in 2003. Thus, some very significant MIT alumni firms were NOT included in the database, such as Arthur D. Little, AMP, Campbell Soup, Genentech, Hewlett-Packard, Intel, McDonnell Douglas, Raytheon, Rockwell, and Texas Instruments because the MIT founder or co-founder had died in all these cases. These omissions illustrate the importance of the scale factor we employed to produce an accurate estimate that partially compensates for the many firms explicitly omitted.

This scaling method rests upon three assumptions. One is that the proportion of entrepreneurs among the respondents is the same as the proportion of entrepreneurs among the non-respondents. The second is that the respondent entrepreneurs are equally successful as the non-respondent entrepreneurs. The proportion of entrepreneurs among the non-respondents (or their success level) could just as easily be higher as it could be lower than the proportion among the respondents. The third is that, for entrepreneurs who started more than one company, then on average the performance of their former or subsequent firms is similar to the firm we observe.

Let us consider how wrong we might be in these estimates. The effect of cutting our scale factor by two (which would represent the extreme case where twice as many respondents as non-respondents were entrepreneurs, or where respondent entrepreneurs were twice as successful as non-respondents) generates the results that are in the conservative wording we chose to use in the introduction of this report:

> ... *if the active companies founded by living MIT graduates formed an independent nation, conservative estimates indicate that their revenues would make that nation at least the seventeenth-largest economy in the world.*

Under these circumstances we would be estimating that 12,900 active companies created by living MIT alumni employ 1.6 million people and have annual world sales of $1 trillion. That is roughly equal to a gross domestic product of \$500 billion, a little less than the GDP of the Netherlands and more than the GDP of Turkey (2006 International Monetary Fund, nominal GDP — not purchasing power parity).

A.5 Comparison of MIT Alumni Firms and US Nationally-Representative Firms (Using the Kauffman Firm Survey)

To determine how the firms created by MIT alumni differ from a nationally-representative sample of entrepreneurial firms, we used the Kauffman Firm Survey (KFS), a panel study of 4928 businesses founded in 2004 and tracked each following year. We downloaded the data set from the Kauffman Foundation web site (http://www.kauffman.org/kfs/), which includes data on these firms through 2008. To compare these "Kauffman firms" with a sample of firms of the same age founded by MIT alumni, we used a subset of the MIT firms where we also had data on the first four years of their operation.

The first observation we made was that the MIT alumni firms were more concentrated in certain industry sectors than the KFS firms, so to fairly compare their performance, we also had to control for industry. To do this, we classified the MIT data set into the industries specified in the Kauffman study as follows:

MIT industries

Professional, Management, and Educational Services includes: *"Architecture," "Law, Accounting, Miscellaneous Business," "Management & Finance Consulting,"* and *"Software"*

Manufacturing includes: *"Aerospace," "Chemicals, Materials," "Consumer Products," "Drugs, Biotech, Medical Devices," "Electronics, Computers, Telecommunications," "Machinery,"* and *"Other Manufacturing"*

Finance and Insurance includes: *"Finance"*

Information includes: *"Publishing, Schools"* and *"Telecommunications"*

Utilities includes: *"Energy Electric Utilities"*

Other includes: *"Other Services"*'

Kauffman industries

The industry categories include companies with the corresponding NAIC code

Other includes companies with NAIC codes not corresponding to any of the other five industry categories.

We then limited the KFS data to those firms in industries that overlapped with the MIT alumni firms. Once we had a subsample from

Variable	Founding year	2nd year	3rd year	4th year	5th year
Founding team size					
MIT mean	2.4	2.3	2.7	2.5	2.2
kauffman mean	1.4	1.5	1.5	1.5	1.5
T-statistic	4.129***	4.437***	7.686***	5.144***	2.981***
Number of employees					
MIT mean	10.4	6.5	11.2	13.8	8.3
Kauffman mean	1.6	2.9	3.0	3.2	3.2
T-statistic	7.873***	3.494***	9.861***	8.880***	3.968***
Revenue (we took the natural log of the firm revenues)					
MIT mean	2.0	2.9	2.7	3.2	2.8
Kauffman mean	1.6	2.1	2.2	2.3	2.3
T-statistic	1.026	3.067***	1.943***	3.549***	1.776***
VC funded					
MIT mean	0.100	0.042	0.372	0.240	0.091
Kauffman Mean	0.018	0.013	0.012	0.007	0.006
T-statistic	1.898*	1.176	16.754***	11.109***	4.343***

***, **, and * indicate statistical significance at the 1%, 5%, and 10% levels, respectively.

the MIT and KFS data sets of matched industries and firm ages, we ran t-tests of means to compare the founding team size, number of employees, revenues and rates of venture capital (VC) funding from the founding year all the way to the fifth year of the firm's operation. We find that the MIT companies had larger founding teams, more employees, higher revenues, and were significantly more likely to be VC funded. However, we did not control for anything other than firm age and broad industry in these *t*-tests.

A.6   MIT Teams Comparison

To further test how the firms created by MIT alumni may differ, we examined the characteristics of firms started by teams of primarily MIT alumni with founding teams consisting of mostly non-MIT alumni. We compare MIT teams that had at least two co-founders. To do this, we classified the founding teams into either "MIT Heavy" or "MIT Light" according to the following method:

MIT Heavy: >50% of founding team were MIT alumni

MIT Light: ≤50% of founding team were MIT alumni

In the following table, we use median tests because outliers might affect the results. Overall, MIT-Heavy teams underperformed MIT-Light teams when no control for the founding team size is used. However, once we controlled for the founding team size, the median comparisons were no longer significant, indicating that the outperformance of the MIT-light teams was mostly due to the larger founding team size. In fact, the table shows that teams with more co-founders have significantly higher revenues, raise more initial capital, and have a higher number of employees. Together with the results above in comparison with the nationally-representative Kauffman Firm Survey, these results indicate that the MIT alumni firms tend to be more likely to raise venture capital, employ more people and generate more revenues than the "average" new US firm. At least some of this difference is likely due to the larger founding team size of the MIT alumni ventures in addition to the training and reputation gained from MIT.

Variable/founding team size	MIT light median	MIT heavy median	Pearson chi-squared
Log (Revenue)			
No control	14.659	13.777	16.207***
Two founders	14.531	13.895	1.317
Three founders	14.876	14.570	0.656
Four founders	14.493	15.774	1.059
Log (initial capital)			
No control	11.513	10.820	8.914***
Two founders	11.918	11.513	0.481
Three	13.122	12.377	0.988
Four	11.513	14.557	1.053
Number of employees			
No control	20.000	9.000	13.061***
Two	18.000	17.500	0.001
Three	25.000	35.000	1.765
Four	15.000	45.000	0.005
Survival (years)			
No control	7.000	7.000	0.000
Two	7.000	6.000	1.822
Three	6.000	7.500	1.379
Four	9.500	4.000	1.833

***, **, and * indicate statistical significance at the 1%, 5%, and 10% levels, respectively.

References

Acs, Z., W. Parsons, and S. Tracy (2008), *High-Impact Firms: Gazelles Revisited*. Washington D.C.: U.S. Small Business Administration, June 2008, Report No. 328.

Association of University Technology Managers (2007), *U.S. Licensing Activity Survey: FY 2006*. Privately Published.

Burt, R. S. (2001), 'Attachment, decay and social network'. *Journal of Organizational Behavior* **22**(6), 619–643.

Chase Manhattan Corporation (1990), *MIT Entrepreneurship in Silicon Valley*. Privately Published, April.

Cooper, A. C. (1986), 'Entrepreneurship and high technology'. In: D. L. Sexton and R. W. Smilor (eds.): *The Art and Science of Entrepreneurship*. Cambridge, MA: Ballinger Publishing, pp. 153–167.

Dobrev, S. D. (2005), 'Career mobility and job flocking'. *Social Science Research* **34**(4), 800–820.

Dobrev, S. D. and W. P. Barnett (2005), 'Organizational roles and transition to entrepreneurship'. *Academy of Management Journal* **48**(3), 433–449.

Dorfman, N. S. (1983), 'Route 128: The development of a regional high technology economy'. *Research Policy* **12**, 299–316.

Eesley, C. E. (2011), 'Alumni surveys as a data collection methodology'. Working Paper. Available at: http://www.stanford.edu/~cee/Papers/Eesley_Alumni_surveys.pdf.

Hsu, D., E. Roberts, and C. Eesley (2007), 'Entrepreneurs from technology-based universities: Evidence from MIT'. *Research Policy* **36**, 768–788.

Jolly, R. W., L. Yu, and P. Orazem (2009), 'After they graduate: An overview of the Iowa State University Alumni Survey'. Iowa State University Economics Working Paper Series # 09002.

Lazear, E. P. (2004), 'Balanced skills and entrepreneurship'. *American Economic Review* **94**(2), 208–211.

Lerner, J. and U. Malmendier (2009), 'With a little help from my (random) friends: Success and failure in post-business school entrepreneurship'. Harvard Business School Working Paper.

Putt, W. D. (ed.) (1974), *How to Start Your Own Business.* Cambridge, MA: The MIT Press and the MIT Alumni Association.

Rich, S. (1985), *Business Plans that Win $$$s: Lessons from the MIT Enterprise Forum.* Cambridge, MA: The MIT Press.

Roberts, E. B. (1991), *Entrepreneurs in High Technology: Lessons from MIT and Beyond.* New York: Oxford University Press.

Schumpeter, J. A. (1936), *The Theory of Economic Development.* Cambridge, MA: Harvard University Press, p. 198.

Summit Consulting (2009), 'Toward effective education of innovative entrepreneurs in small business: Initial results from a survey of college students and graduates'. SBA Office of Advocacy. Available at http://archive.sba.gov/advo/research/rs353tot.pdf.

Wadhwa, V., A. Saxenian, B. Rissing, and G. Gereffi (2007), 'America's new immigrant entrepreneurs: Part I (January 4, 2007)'. Duke Science, Technology & Innovation Paper No. 23. Available at SSRN: http://ssrn.com/abstract=990152.

Ziegler, C. A. (1982), 'Looking at glass houses: A study of fissioning in an innovative science-based firm'. Unpublished Ph.D. Dissertation. Waltham, MA: Brandeis University.

CPSIA information can be obtained at www.ICGtesting.com
Printed in the USA
BVOW11s1726270515

401960BV00003B/30/P